THE WORST THING

THE WORST THING

A.M. YOUNG

NEW DEGREE PRESS

THE WORST THING

ISBN   978-1-63676-371-2   *Paperback*

          978-1-63676-449-8   *Kindle Ebook*

          978-1-63676-372-9   *Ebook*

For Tyler, duh.

CONTENTS

"Of course he wasn't dead. He could never be dead until she herself had finished feeling and thinking."

—ZORA NEALE HURSTON

AUTHOR'S NOTE

You'd think that the biggest changes in life would take time or be accompanied by a dramatic flair, but in reality, they happen quickly and almost without a whisper. One moment Tyler was alive, the next he was not. One moment my phone was ringing, the next I was on the floor screaming. The entire fabric and course of my life changed almost instantly with just a few words, setting everything into disarray and horror. Tyler spent years working, fighting, struggling to beat addiction and regain a healthy life, but it was all wiped away in a moment.

There was a time when I waited for the news of his death every day. I had seen him at what we then thought was his rock bottom. We were constantly worrying about him with genuine uncertainty about his chances of survival. For a year and a half, he was in recovery and came out the other side a more mature and emotionally secure person with a high school degree and a readiness to leave his past in the past to take on the world. COVID-19 sent him back under our roof where we could watch him, and he seemed like he was doing well. We slowly started to breathe again and regain some of our hope. How suddenly this effort and hope were extinguished, disappearing into the night alongside Tyler's soul.

After the complete devastation and unreality of Tyler's death began to fade, I realized that his story, while deeply personal and tragic for our family and friends, is not unique. The opioid crisis is recent and expanding, with Oxycontin's debut on the market in the 1990s and fentanyl's appearance in illegal drug communities in 2017. The drug that killed my brother is fifty to one hundred times stronger than pure morphine, and it has wreaked havoc on communities across America in the three short years since it entered the picture, to the tune of 31,000+ deaths per year and rising (Centers for Disease Control, 2021).

This crisis is only recently being taken seriously by the federal government; in October 2020, after I began writing this book, Purdue Pharma was finally forced to settle criminal and civil investigations for $8 billion (Mann, 2020). Their false advertising, fudged statistics, and illegal marketing campaigns sowed the seeds of destruction across families of all races, ethnicities, religions, geographic locations, and socioeconomic statuses (Macy, 2018).

While this sliver of justice is promising, so much damage is already done, and stigma against addiction is still equally rampant and devastating. Part of my mission in writing this book is to tackle these stereotypes that prevent the victims of the opioid crisis from healing. My brother, an upper-middle class white kid with a good education and a loving family in the suburbs of Washington, DC, was not an anomaly, and I am not ashamed of him. He struggled with addiction and mental health issues for most of his life, and he ultimately lost a battle against an illness that was out of his control.

In writing this book, I want to use my own personal experience to paint a broader picture of mental health and addiction. I want to explore the intimate, unique details of Tyler's case to show the common themes of addiction and help people understand how something like this happens. Addiction is an equal-opportunity nightmare, and by telling Tyler's story, I hope to educate others on how the unimaginable becomes reality.

I want this book to be a memorial, a celebration of life, a eulogy, a relatable story, a lesson, and a warning. I want to help myself and my loved ones heal from our immeasurable loss by remembering the goofy blond kid we know and love, but I also want to connect with others who never met him and never will. I want those with addiction, those who love someone with addiction, those who are grieving, and those who feel lost to understand that they are not alone.

And while the opioid crisis looks bleak and the largeness of the problem is daunting, it does create a network of solidarity. Loss of this magnitude is truly a shitty club that no one wants to be in, but it's the most supportive and helpful club one could ever join. I have felt so embraced by those around me since Tyler passed, and I have a deep desire to pay it forward and send my own messages of comfort and empathy into the world.

However, I sincerely wish to connect with those who did not know my brother. His story highlights an issue that affects everyone, for even if you have never been personally affected by substance abuse or mental health issues, your community has. It should not take a personal, life-changing tragedy to spread awareness of the problem, and quite frankly, I don't want more people to be able to relate. Only through sharing our stories and educating can we get ahead of the problem before it is too late. I do not wish this pain on anyone, and if writing this book saves even one life or educates even one person on how to help those who are struggling, it was more than worth it.

But mostly, this book is for Tyler. While these stories of loss are so common, they are each uniquely painful and irreplaceable. Everyone has a way of remembering their loved one, and this is mine. There are so many things Tyler will never be able to do, so I see it as my job to carry his legacy onward. After all, I am the only person on this planet who shares all his DNA. I spent nineteen years loving someone who was fighting an invisible battle every day of his life; I was fighting a different but greatly painful battle alongside him. In his absence, who better to tell his story than me?

I chose to write this book immediately after his death, which shocked many of my friends and family members. Many worried that it was too soon, that maybe I should wait until my grief was more settled and I had some space between me and the event to reflect. I disagree, though, and I think the urgency with which I wrote this book is what makes it so powerful. You are experiencing my emotions in real time, as I feel them, following my journey of discovering what happened and processing my own emotions. I am not reflecting back years later after I have healed and made sense of everything; I am exposing the true and powerful rawness of the worst thing that ever happens to people.

I cannot promise you a happy ending within these pages— that is up to us as soon as the book is closed. There is no happy ending for Tyler, but there can be for someone else if we can keep Tyler's memory alive, educate ourselves and others, and fight the good fight.

I

———

Leesburg, Virginia, August 17, 2020. A Monday morning, the day was unseasonably nice—Virginia summers can often reach oppressive humidity and temperatures in the high 90s. My mom and stepdad, Jeff, decided to make the back porch their office for the day, setting up their laptops on the shaded table.

Around 11:50 a.m., my mom decided that it was time to wake up my younger brother, Tyler. He was nineteen years old, so sleeping until noon was nothing out of the ordinary.

She set her coffee mug down on the kitchen island as she walked back inside the house. As she made her way up the stairs and down the back hallway toward Tyler's room, her mind was filled with the to-do list of things they needed to prepare for his upcoming departure. That day in particular, he needed to call his asthma doctor to schedule an appointment before he flew back to Chicago for college on Friday. He needed a new inhaler prescription, and my mom did not want him traveling without it, especially while COVID-19 cases were skyrocketing across the country.

When she got to his door, her knock was met with no response. Typical Tyler, sleeping the morning away. She opened the door to total darkness and the fan whirring, just as he usually kept his room. She flipped on the light switch and walked toward the bed.

"Time to get up," she said cheerily. "It's almost noon. You have to call your asthma doctor today—hopefully, she can get you in this week on such late notice."

But he did not stir. Usually by this point he was at least sitting up, groggily rubbing his eyes or whining for her to get out of his room. She made her way across the room to his bed, wondering why he wasn't responding. Even a deep sleep would have been ruined at this point with so much light and noise.

As she stood over him, she could clearly see something was wrong. He was not moving at all, lying on his side facing away from her. His head rested on his right arm, which extended beneath him. The position itself was not alarming, but then she saw the coloring of his arm: blotched and purple from the fingers all the way to where his arm disappeared into his sleeve.

"Tyler?" she whispered, shaking his shoulder. She immediately felt the stiff heaviness of his arm. It was already cold.

My stepdad was still on the porch when he heard my mom's shouting voice coming from inside. He couldn't hear what she was saying, but she was clearly worked up about something, so he opened the back door to figure out what was going on. My mom was flying down the staircase.

"TYLER'S DEAD!" came the bone-chilling scream, which she then repeated over and over. Jeff stood there for a moment, completely stunned. She grabbed him, practically pushing him up the stairs. "GO!"

"Call 911!" Jeff screamed back once his brain began to process, and he started running up the stairs two at a time. Speeding down the hall, he knew something was wildly wrong but figured there was still a fighting chance. Tyler wasn't actually dead; surely, he had messed up, overdosed on a drug, gone a little too far this time, but the ambulance would come, and the paramedics would get him back to normal.

On the phone, the 911 operator similarly didn't seem to think that Tyler could actually be dead. She asked several frustrating, time-consuming questions about what my mom had seen while she kept screaming back at her, begging her to send someone already. They finally agreed to dispatch an ambulance but kept asking more protocol questions. While they were just regulatory background questions to determine what was happening, they enraged my helpless mom who knew what she had just seen.

A moment later, Jeff descended the stairs, more slowly this time. He immediately embraced my mom, simply saying, "I'm sorry. I'm sorry." It was this defeated phrase, his lack of urgency, the admission that there was nothing else they could do, that confirmed to my mom what she already knew, and sent her over the edge. She and Jeff held each other, sobbing, and trying not to panic while they waited for the first responders.

When she collected herself enough to speak, my mom walked out onto the front porch and called my dad. My parents, divorced but great partners in co-parenting, lived about two miles down the road from each other. My dad was rarely attentive to his phone, so he missed my mom's first call and tried her back a few minutes later.

"Hello?" he answered. He surprised my mom, who was not mentally ready to tell him the news but had no choice.

"Tyler's *dead!*" she gasped through tears, for lack of any other way to say it.

"What?!" my dad yelped, his voice breaking. "*Where is he?*"

"In his bed," she responded, barely choking the words out.

"NO!" my dad was screaming. "NO! NO!"

My mom heard background noise, movement, and my stepmom, Lindsey, asking what was happening as my dad continued to yell, his words indiscernible.

"I'm coming right over," he finally managed and hung up the phone.

She was forced to repeat the same phone call with me. Eerily, I reacted almost identically to my dad.

I was across the country in my Los Angeles apartment, making my morning mug of tea between my first and second meetings of the day. When she called me, I did not think anything was out of the ordinary—my mom and I are close, often talking on the phone several times a day. That day, though, as soon as I heard her voice, I knew she was not calling for idle chitchat.

"Hey momma," I answered.

My mother replied with an incomprehensible, distorted whimper.

"Mom?" I asked, my stomach turning.

"Tyler's dead," she whispered, barely able to speak.

Just like my dad, I immediately asked where he was, then told her I too, was on my way. The only difference between my dad and I was that I had a couple minutes of complete shock in which I called my boss to relay the news. I simply told her what had happened and sat motionless until she told me to take all the time I needed and urged me to hang up the phone. Then, just as my father had, I fell to the floor, screaming "NO!" in my own chant of horrified disbelief.

In a moment, my roommate was rocking me back and forth while she searched for the next flight from Los Angeles to Dulles International Airport.

Back in Virginia, the paramedics finally arrived at my mom's house. They rushed upstairs with life-saving equipment in tow, but just like Jeff, returned downstairs slowly, almost reluctantly, as they knew the news they had to declare.

"I'm sorry," one of them said to my mom as he came down, just like Jeff had.

My dad, who had arrived at some point during the chaos, shoved past them and ran toward Tyler's room himself, still unable to believe what was happening. The medics tried to stop him, but he demanded to see his son with his own eyes.

After these initial moments of horror, my parents set up camp in the dining room. There was a flurry of activity as the paramedics did a preliminary examination and the police searched the room and asked the first questions of the unfolding investigation.

"Ma'am," one of them asked my mom, who was at this moment sitting in numb silence. "Where were you last night?"

"Wha … what?" my mom turned to him in pure confusion.

Since he was only nineteen years old and there was no obvious cause of death, they had to treat the situation like a potential homicide. While my mom understood this and appreciated their due diligence, being treated like a potential homicide suspect mere minutes after finding her son's dead body was beyond human comprehension.

The paramedics called a chaplain who arrived and stayed the rest of the afternoon. Coincidentally, he came from my stepmom, Lindsey's, church, the same church that would later host Tyler's funeral. Once Lindsey had also arrived at my mom's house, he gathered my four parents, linking their hands in the dining room and leading prayers for Tyler, offering emotional support, and generally saying all the right things. When it was time to move the body into the ambulance, he led my mom to the backyard so she wouldn't have to watch. At the last minute, she changed her mind—she wanted to say one last goodbye before the body went for the autopsy.

The group walked out onto the driveway, at this point brimming with ambulances and police cars. My parents put their hands on the makeshift casket, a sort of white box with a blanket over top, and let the chaplain say one final prayer. The whole time, my mother was laser-focused on the activity in front of her, but weeks later, she stood on the front porch, looking out at the street beyond our driveway where the emergency vehicles had parked, and thought of how incredibly awful the whole scene had looked. She wondered if any neighbors drove past at that bleak moment and saw her praying over her son's body.

When the 911 responders and chaplain left, it was time to do the unpleasant work of spreading the news. Jeff drove off to his ex-wife's house to tell his three children, my stepsiblings, what had happened. Lindsey's older two kids were not in town, so she had to make the announcement via phone calls. She also had to begin thinking of how to tell my five-year-old brother. My mom called me again, finally having a moment to think and see how I was handling things (not very well). My mind couldn't seem to comprehend what was going on, so I used this shock and inability to freak the fuck out to my advantage and organized my return home. By the time she called for the second time, I was already boarding at LAX and gave her my flight information so someone could pick me up when I landed. Reassured of my safety and itinerary, she then hung up to tell other close friends and family members.

I arrived at Dulles Airport around 10:30 that night. Jeff was there to pick me up, and he drove us the short distance back to my mom's house, under my rapid fire of questions that he could not answer. As soon as I entered the house, I beelined for my mom and dad. The three of us hugged each other, and I felt the most bizarre sensation that I was now the only thing connecting these two people who had once been a family.

Then we began preparing for the funeral.

We now know that Tyler's cause of death was acute fentanyl poisoning, or accidental overdose. Fentanyl is an incredibly strong synthetic opioid that became popular in 2017, hitting the streets and creating a gold mine for dealers. It is fifty to one hundred times stronger than morphine and can be mixed with other street drugs like heroin and cocaine, or illegal prescription pills. It is cheap and potent, meaning bigger profits for dealers and stronger highs for users—if it doesn't kill them first (Macy, 2018).

By 2017, the opioid epidemic was already in its third decade. Starting with the overprescribing and underreporting side effects of prescription painkillers like Oxycontin, opioid addiction swept the country and did not discriminate based on age, gender, race or ethnicity, or even socio-economic background. Virginia was a hotspot for opioid abuse as old coal mining towns in Appalachia produced thousands of ex-miners with chronic pain. Doctors at the time were incentivized to prescribe the drug by the drug's manufacturer, Purdue Pharma, which offered gear, fancy dinners, and even luxury vacations disguised as an informational retreat. Legal prescription turned into illegal abuse and addiction spread well beyond the initial targets of those with pain needs. In the 2010s, as the FDA cracked down on drug advertising and prescribing, street opioids like heroin became more common. Those who were already addicted to pills, their supply potentially being cut short, could switch to heroin, and new users could now escalate more quickly as heroin became more abundant than pills. (Macy, 2018).

I spoke with a former detective, now sergeant, in the county's narcotics unit, to try to understand how this happened. My family lives in Loudoun County, a suburb of Washington, DC. Loudoun has the highest median income of any county in the country, but neither the proximity to the city nor the abundant wealth protects its inhabitants from the opioid epidemic. In fact, most of the illicit opioids in the area come directly from DC or Baltimore, widely considered the heroin capital of the United States (Beatty, 2016). While the county itself is not a manufacturing source, the city hub is only thirty minutes away.

The fentanyl that matriculates from DC into Loudoun is primarily sourced from China or Mexico. Chinese fentanyl tends to be more potent (i.e., deadly), sometimes reaching 95 percent purity. Mexican fentanyl is typically around 40 percent pure, but even that concentration can easily kill a user. With any illegal drug purchase, there is never a certainty about where the drug comes from. Heroin or pills you buy on the street could easily be laced with fentanyl, or even be only fentanyl. Since it is a strong opioid, it has the same effect. Dealers will often cut more expensive substances with fentanyl to increase potency while saving money and are not concerned with consequential overdoses. In fact, a customer's overdose increases sales as it lets other addicted users know that this dealer's product is strong (Macy, 2018).

An addicted brain is wired to do anything in its power to avoid withdrawal symptoms, even if it means buying something that might kill you. As users gain a tolerance, they require more of a drug to keep them from getting sick, making fentanyl a realistic endpoint for users who started with weaker opioids like heroin or prescription pills. It is not an active choice but a disease, and by the time a user's brain craves something as strong as fentanyl, it is incredibly challenging to turn back. Taking a potentially lethal opioid is not the only drastic measure an addicted person will take to avoid withdrawal symptoms. Drug-related robberies, assaults, and homicides also "develop together" with increased opioid use in affected communities (Hammersley, Forsyth, Morrison, and Davies, 1989).

It is unclear what Tyler thought he was doing when he took the fentanyl-laced pill that killed him. He bought it from a dealer acquaintance he had purchased from before, and based on text messages, knew it was a strong opioid. He did not think it was lethal, though. The dealer messaged him the day before he died telling him to be careful—he had tried a pill from the same batch and overdosed but lived. Based on what detectives found in Tyler's phone, he was just beginning to experiment with opioids, but he was not yet addicted. His substance abuse issues up to that point had not included much opioid abuse; the most frightening substances we knew he had used at that point were benzodiazepines like Xanax or methamphetamines. He took the pill as an introduction to opioids, but his first sample ended up being his last.

Loudoun County typically sees fewer than twenty drug overdoses a year, but the startling majority of these deaths are of young adults under thirty years old. One of the first times I visited Tyler's grave, a man whose son is buried nearby told me about the surrounding occupants.

"That one was twenty-five, fentanyl," he sighed, pointing to a headstone a few rows behind Tyler's. He kept pointing. "Eighteen, fentanyl. Twenty-three, fentanyl. Twenty, suicide.

Twenty-four, fentanyl. My son was twenty-six, did some cocaine that he didn't know was laced with fentanyl."

This corner of the cemetery, full of young drug overdoses, exists in every county across the United States. Tyler's death is deeply personal and tragic, but it is also a statistic. He is part of a much larger problem that has been haunting the country for three decades, ripping families apart regardless of where they live, how much money they make, or how well they raise their kids. While Tyler's story is intimate and unique, it should also be used as a warning to others, a tale of caution of how the worst thing that can ever happen to a family actually happens.

II

_____

Most people who know what happened to our family primarily worry about my mom. Virtually every phone call or text I received after the initial outreach that comes after death either started or ended with, "How's your mom?" She still has the most people sending her flowers, checking up on her, and stopping by the house for lunch.

On the pyramid of grief, losing a child is typically considered right at the top: the worst loss a person can endure. I'm sure most people who are childless like me have at some point done something dangerous and received a parental lecture about how stressful it is to be worried about a child. After making any sort of trouble in high school, I would always hear something along the lines of, "You don't even know how deeply you are capable of loving another human being until you make your own!" I have no way of knowing if this is true or not yet, but I certainly don't doubt it. Tyler, as my only full sibling, is the person I love most in the world, the deepest love I have ever known, and I would imagine my already overwhelming loss would be even more intense if he had literally grown inside of me, come out of me, and was at one point a part of my own body.

Because of this cultural idea that has been drilled into my brain, I also worry about my mom endlessly. I watched her bury her own child, a twisted role reversal that is the fuel of nightmares for mothers around the world. Even in her best moments, I can't help but be terrified of the repercussions of her immeasurable loss. She is incredibly strong—I do not think she will waste away without a sense of purpose, nor do I think she would ever hurt herself. Still, it is foreign territory for all of us, and that unconditional love I have heard so much about is powerful enough to render many parents completely crushed in the wake of such a tragedy. She is now *a mother who has lost her child*, a pitiful fact that will remain with her until she herself leaves this Earth.

Weirdly enough, my mom predicted this awful fate a few years before it happened. Her ominous fortune telling had nothing to do with the increasing severity of Tyler's own struggles—it did not follow the logical pattern of, "the more Tyler struggles, the more likely it is he will die." Instead, a completely unrelated event triggered this cryptic, unwanted prophecy that plagued her mind until the morning of August 17.

In 2018, one of our neighbor's sons passed away. When my mom detailed this story to me those years ago, her eyes were wide with morbid fascination. It was not the fascination of a gossiper, though—it was the fascination of someone who was empathizing in a strange, unknown way.

"I cannot imagine how she is possibly surviving this," my mom said, shaking her head. What she didn't vocalize was the ominous feeling of dread that settled in her heart. Since that moment, she had been harboring a secret prediction that she, too, would one day have to bury her own son.

At that time, I could not see inside my mother's head or understand such a horrible thought. Of course, as a child with substance abuse issues, Tyler and his safety and well-being were constantly in question, but for your own mother to have a hunch that you were going to die was spooky, to put it lightly. Perhaps it was part of the motherly intuition I don't yet understand, but it seemed as if my mom had some supernatural knowledge that only a mother can possess. She wasn't able to explain it to me any better than, "I just know," and quite frankly, I'm not sure I want to understand.

This premonition, while exceedingly creepy, did ultimately help my mother cope when Tyler's death became a reality. Unlike me, who clung on to a blind security in Tyler's future, my mom had already contemplated the possible end to Tyler's story. After his death, she grasped the positives more quickly than I had expected. While I never really considered the horrible "what if," my mom had watched her friend go through it and started to prepare herself. She had witnessed another mother survive the worst-case scenario and come out the other side wounded but grateful for the short and beautiful life of her own son. I truly believe our neighbor's resilience acted as a guiding star for her, showing her the possibility to move forward and keep Tyler's memory alive. I previously considered her contemplation and internalization of our neighbor's accident as a morbid obsession, but in hindsight I almost feel like she was pre-grieving. She had seen it done before and was well armed against the hardest parts with a map to the good parts.

Months after Tyler's death, I don't think she is anywhere close to the final stage of full acceptance, yet shortly after his death, she was more ready than I expected to find ways to make her own life still meaningful and celebrate Tyler's memory. I fully thought I would have to motivate her to get out of bed every day or give her constant pep talks about how to move forward, but she possesses an unparalleled ability to stay positive. Since Tyler's death, she has raised tens of thousands of dollars for addicted kids in need and even received a promotion at work. Her life is by no means spiraling out of control, and I can't take credit for any of these accomplishments. One day a few short months after the funeral, I asked her how she was feeling. Her response outright shocked me.

"I'm so thankful," she said through tears, but with a genuine smile. "I am so lucky that God chose me to be Tyler's mom. Not everyone would be strong enough to handle a child with Tyler's struggles, but God saw that I could and chose me. He could have given me an easy kid or a boring kid, but I am so thankful I got to be *Tyler's* mom."

The physical embodiment of the phrase, "Don't cry because it's over, smile because it happened," my mom has embraced the sorrow while still holding the good times in her heart. She recognizes that it only hurts so bad now because Tyler was so special, and their relationship was so strong. Neither my mom nor I would ever trade those nineteen years with Tyler for eighty years with any other son/brother. Knowing this, my mom wakes up every day and chooses to focus on the happiness we had instead of the potential we lost.

––––––––––––––––––

My mom did not have an easy go of raising her second child. Tyler was always a fundamentally active person, always on the move, thinking, learning, and getting into things. Even as an infant, he required constant attention—he escaped from his crib several times before his first birthday. When we first moved from the Chicago suburbs to northern Virginia (my parents were still married at this point—they split when I was eleven, Tyler seven), a few neighbors came over to introduce themselves and deliver housewarming gifts. Hardly any of our furniture or belongings had been delivered to the house yet, so my mom redirected everyone to the spacious, wooded backyard. As my mom was giving the grand tour, she suddenly realized that much like the living room couches, her two-year-old son was also not in attendance.

The house sat on three acres of land with dense forest in all directions, full of ways for a toddler to get hurt. Immediately panicking, my mom and the neighbors who were with her began a frantic search for Tyler. The number of potential dangers and hiding places in those woods was infinite, and terror spread as the three acres were scoured to no avail. Finally, she decided to run back through the house to the front porch and alert my dad, who was chatting with the husbands.

She flung open the back door and stopped in her tracks. There was little Tyler, sitting on the kitchen floor, a cleaning supply bottle in his chubby hands and bleach all over the tile and carpet.

"Hi Mommy!" he waved in innocent toddler bliss. He pointed to the bleach stains he had created on the floor. "I clean here, and I clean here, and I clean here…"

A few years later when he was six and I was ten, our dad took us fishing at a pond in a nearby park. My nose suddenly started bleeding, so my mom picked me up, leaving Tyler with my dad. Just like at our housewarming event, Tyler was there one moment, gone the next. This incident was even more terrifying than the last, as the presence of a large body of water presented the possibility of drowning. My mom raced back to the pond with me, dialing 911. We finally found

Tyler wandering a half mile away through town completely alone, nonchalantly searching for my mom and me.

This pattern of independent curiosity pervaded through his entire childhood and adolescence. To me, Tyler was always the hyper, incredibly annoying little brother, and to my parents, he was quite a handful. As he grew older and learned more about the world, the types of trouble he got into changed, but his restless nature never diminished. His pediatrician thought he might have ADHD, realizing years later that he had the exact opposite issue: he could laser focus on anything for hours if he was interested, his mind just seemed to be operating on full speed at all times.

Later diagnoses confirmed that Tyler and I suffered from many of the same mental struggles, his just more intense than mine. We both have hyperactive minds generating anxiety and obsessive-compulsive disorder. The main difference between us was how we coped with these issues. Tyler's problems were much more debilitating than mine, not easily quelled by antidepressants and cognitive behavioral therapy. His stress and intrusive thoughts would sometimes render him completely exhausted or overwhelmed. This constant racing in his mind led him to search for ways to numb himself, to calm his brain through synthetic means. My parents tried every sort of counseling and medication recommended to them by doctors, but nothing worked well enough to ease Tyler's mind. Only when he was older and gained some emotional maturity through therapy and rehab could he even vocalize this need and explain his troubles.

Illicit substances first entered the story when Tyler was a young teenager. He began experimenting with marijuana and alcohol, which was concerning although not terribly scandalous. Our older stepbrother, Connor, had also snuck a beer and smoked a joint in high school. At the time, Tyler's behavior was still in the "normal" territory, and nobody thought it would have lifelong ramifications. It was just a phase—he would mature and grow out of it.

Especially alongside Tyler's academic and extracurricular accomplishments, his mischief seemed manageable. He was breezing through college-level math classes in high school, attending summer camps at Princeton, Yale, and UCLA, joining the National Honor Society, and participating in extracurriculars like marching band and cross country. He had friends and girlfriends and got good grades (if he remembered to do his homework). For all his misdemeanors, it seemed to my parents that he was developing normally. It was just a quirk, my crazy but genius little brother who caused mischief while making everyone laugh. Tyler's troublemaking was also never malicious, another factor that disarmed the whole family from worrying too much about him. He never intended to hurt anyone. Instead, his crimes were motivated by curiosity or his own entertainment. For so long, he simply just did not fit the archetype of an addict.

My mom recognizes the turning point as Thanksgiving of 2017, when Tyler was sixteen years old. I was studying abroad in London, but the rest of my mom's family was visiting my stepdad's relatives near Dallas. The trip had gone well until the last day when they were packing to return home. My mom came into the room that Tyler was sharing with our stepbrother, Dalton, to see how they were doing. Tyler was acting suspiciously, darting his eyes at his suitcase, and avoiding my mom's gaze.

"Tyler," my mom sighed, knowing something was going on. "What's in the suitcase?"

"Nothing!" he retorted the panic clear in his voice.

"Open the suitcase, Tyler," she demanded.

When he finally did, she found a stolen, expired prescription bottle. She and Jeff went into the bathroom to see where he had found the bottle and discovered even more evidence of some sort of bender—the toilet paper holder was broken, and there was an empty liquor bottle hidden in the bottom of the trashcan. After much probing, they finally got Dalton to admit that Tyler had gotten drunk by himself the night before, which alarmed my mom more than the substances themselves. This was not drinking as a fun social activity, but something Tyler did by himself, in private. Almost…like an addict.

She confronted him, and he immediately broke down in tears.

"Mom," he sobbed. "I haven't been sober in a year."

This was the pivotal moment in my mom's mind where Tyler transformed from a troublesome kid to a young adult with a serious substance abuse issue. We knew that he had been using drugs and alcohol in the year leading up to this moment, yet still considering it no more than teenage experimentation. Now, however, an invisible line had been crossed, and Tyler's issues could no longer be categorized as immaturity. Things escalated quickly from that point, as mom entered Tyler into intensive therapy, and by March of 2018, he was in his first live-in recovery program. No one came down and bestowed Tyler with the title of Drug Addict. Instead, my mom had to be the one to both recognize the issue and take action on it, no matter how hard it was to accept.

The night Tyler died, my mom slept in my room. We held onto each other, both crying and unable to achieve more than a brief doze. At one point, we both accepted the fact that we were not going to get any real sleep and began talking about how much we missed Tyler.

"Oh, Mom," I hugged her tightly, and tried to think of a way to lighten the mood. "I know he was your favorite."

"Yeah," she sighed, and burst into a joint laugh-cry, the first time any of us had smiled all day.

This joke provided a brief moment of lightheartedness on the worst day of our lives, but when I thought about it later, it made me realize something about my mom's dedication and love for her children.

My mom and I are extremely close. Closer, in fact, than she ever was with Tyler. We talk on the phone several times a day and share everything with each other, which is made possible by the fact that I have not needed her parenting help nearly as much as Tyler did, nor have I ever kept any meaningful secrets from her. Tyler fully tested the limits of her maternal love—something that I have never done. Meanwhile, I sometimes gave her advice of my own—something Tyler was never in a position to do.

Despite this, she never docked points from Tyler for his problems, and she never gave up on him, no matter how many sleepless nights he caused. She never favored me because I was easier to raise, or because our relationship turned into equal parts mother-daughter and best friends. Instead, she poured her entire being into trying to save the child who needed it...while still maintaining a closeness and love with the one who didn't need it. I never suffered from the extra time and attention that she had to give Tyler, nor did I resent either of them for it. Our relationships with our mom are so different, yet equally precious in her heart. I do not believe that she loves Tyler more than me or that he was "the favorite," or that she loved him less because he caused her so much stress. We are *both* the favorite child. She has the completely unbiased ability to love according to our unique personalities.

Whether this is unique to her or part of that motherly love that is so mysterious to me, it's downright honorable.

I am so proud of how she has handled the loss of the younger, favorite child. Objectively, she is doing really poorly—she is still a mother who has lost her child. All that love, time, money, worry, and energy poured into him, and he still didn't make it. Certainly not a waste, but a tragedy. Subjectively, though, given everything that's happened to her, she's doing impressively well. She still stands strong and uses his story as a motivation rather than a handicap. Already, she has committed to dedicating her post-retirement life to helping others who are struggling with addiction. She has raised a memorial fund of over $40,000 and is joining support groups in the effort to heal herself so that one day she will be able to heal others. The motivation she possessed to tangibly love Tyler while he was alive was completely unaffected by his death.

My mom largely credits this strength and drive to one of the strangest coincidences I have ever experienced.

Four days before Tyler died, she, my stepdad, and Dalton were on vacation in South Carolina. I was living in Los Angeles and had a welcome dinner with a friend who just moved to the area. At an overpriced outdoor bar in Culver City, I vented to him about Tyler's situation, which had seemed to improve but still made me nervous. I ranted about his time in rehab, his current lapses in an otherwise promising sobriety, and the constant anxiety I felt about him. Then I stopped myself and apologized—his dad suffered from alcoholism and had passed away when he was young. I felt bad for complaining to someone who had actually seen their loved one die.

"At least Tyler is still alive," I said to my friend on one of the last days this statement would ever be true.

"I don't know, though," he replied. "My dad is gone, but at least I don't have to worry about him anymore. I remember the stress and anxiety of watching someone you love struggle with addiction, and it is not fun. I miss my dad, but I don't have to worry about him anymore. He is at peace, and so am I."

This was such a bizarre concept to me. At the time, I couldn't imagine any positive sides of losing someone you love. I turned this conversation over in my head for the rest of the night. For the next three days, I repeatedly tried to call my mom and discuss the strange feeling my friend had shared, only to have the conversation derailed each time. She was busy deep-sea fishing or lying on a South Carolina beach. Several times I would start talking and be cut off so she could pull up directions on her phone or order at a restaurant. The story went untold, and by the time she called me on Monday to tell me about Tyler, it was completely forgotten.

It was only later that day, once things had settled down, my cross-country travel over, speaking with my mom privately that I had a chance to debrief. What she uttered next was the second most shocking thing I had heard that day.

"This might be weird," she started. "But right when I found him, before I ran downstairs to tell Jeff, before anything else, I felt peace."

"What?" I blinked at her.

"I know, it sounds awful, but the very first thing I felt when I realized what had happened was this inexplicable peace, like Tyler was telling me that he was okay, he wasn't struggling anymore."

I stared at her for a moment before speaking.

"Mom," I said. "That's exactly what I was trying to tell you over the weekend."

This peace, which can only be understood once you have experienced it, has propelled both of us toward acceptance. We are not quite there yet, but we both realize that Tyler's life, while precious and meaningful, was wrought with struggles from the day he was born. Despite having the strongest mom in the world, he was still constantly battling with himself. Now, his fight is over, his problems can harm him no more, he no longer needs dangerous substances just to make it through the day.

It is because of this that my mom is glad she was the one who found him. While it seems horrible, it is better than any alternative. A phone call? Him being a time zone away in Chicago, instead of at home? My mom fully believes that Tyler sent her that peace at the moment of his discovery. This knowledge that he is finally cured of his ailments serves the dual purpose of two things: First, it motivates her to help others who can still be helped. While she is comforted by Tyler's peace, she still realizes that it didn't have to be this way. While many stories of addiction end in this worst-case scenario, others don't. Some people do eventually over-come their sickness and find a living peace that Tyler never achieved. To reach that symbiosis of peace within life is every parent of an addicted child's dream, and just because Tyler is gone, my mom will not stop dreaming for others. Second, this peace lets her know in her heart that, maybe for the first time ever, her younger, favorite child is finally safe and happy.

My mom and I will continue to support one another as we navigate our new reality together. I hope one day, if I have children of my own, I will finally understand how she could possibly be this strong and love us so unconditionally. Until then, I'll continue to stare at her in awe as she lives the rest of her life full of love for her two favorite children.

III

———

Growing up, my dad was a typical guy's guy. He kept up with his sports teams, particularly baseball and football, and coached wrestling at a high school in the area. I was a total daddy's girl. I played baseball for a while, stuck with wrestling all the way through college, and even had a brief stint playing flag football. Tyler, on the other hand, was ushered around from little league sport to sport, nothing ever quite sticking. In an attempt to get him genuinely interested in a sport, he tried tae kwon do, soccer, baseball, football, wrestling, cross country, track, and basketball. Nothing ever landed, though. During wrestling practice in first grade, he would ask to use the bathroom and wander the school, bored, looking for something more interesting to do than wrestling. He didn't fare much better in anything else they made him try.

Tyler was like a space alien. Unlike me, he was fiercely independent, not interested in following in the footsteps of either parent. He was a creature of his own, but that never bothered my dad. While plenty of other parents we knew in the wrestling community seemed to live through their kids, my dad was completely on board with whatever Tyler wanted to do. It seemed like Tyler was from another world in many ways, his own person through and through. Yet my dad, instead of feeling distant from or unable to connect with his son, embraced these differences and became his biggest fan. His hopes for a wrestler son turned into unconditional support for Tyler's trombone playing, math skills, and golf tournaments, even if he didn't have any valuable advice to give. In this way, they cultivated an organic relationship that celebrated their differences. My dad spoke proudly of his son at Yale summer camp while Tyler appreciated the freedom to be himself—the two were truly buddies.

The close relationship they had has naturally made me worry about my dad since he lost Tyler. Especially since his style of grieving is so different than mine, I can never gauge how he's feeling. He does not constantly talk about missing Tyler or visit his gravesite every day. He mentions Tyler in more casual contexts, bringing up a memory when something reminds him or responding whenever our little brother, Hudson, asks about him. Declarations of his sadness are different, though. While my mom finds reminiscing about Tyler and visiting the gravesite comforting, they bring my dad no peace. It completely guts him and leaves him in tears.

One night we were driving home from dinner at my dad and stepmom's favorite pizza place, and we drove past the cemetery. My dad made a chilling comment that might have been the only time I've ever heard him offer a view into his grief.

"Whenever I drive past," my dad murmured, barely above a whisper, "I just wonder if he's cold."

When I finally had a private moment to sit down with my dad and ask him how he was feeling, it all gushed out. I simply asked how he was feeling and sat back to hear what had been running through his mind for months.

"I'm hurting real bad," he said quietly. "I'm still in disbelief. Sometimes I think he's just going to walk through the door."

We talked for a long time, and I was surprised at how similar our struggles were. While we expressed these struggles differently, we were both hung up on a guilt and lack of understanding of how we could have helped Tyler.

My dad and Tyler had both different interests and wildly dissimilar experiences with substance use. My dad, who refused to take his recommended OxyContin prescription after a shoulder surgery because he didn't like the way it made him feel, had never gone further than having a few drinks or trying marijuana with friends. He is social and enjoys a Jack and Coke while maintaining his limits. He also has never experimented with anything hard. He teaches health and physical education, so in theory he is well versed in the signs of addiction, but it's another story when it's in your own household.

"I thought I had seen it all," he said. "But it's different. You don't want to believe it."

Textbook knowledge of drugs is helpful, yet ultimately it did not prepare him for his son's addiction. When it's not clear cut on a page in front of you and your personal feelings and loved ones are on the line, your drug and health education goes out the window. This unfamiliarity with how substance abuse really felt and looked like in person made it difficult for my dad to understand all of Tyler's struggles and needs. He had never suffered from Tyler's anxiety issues, never needed to resort to substances to get through the day and had no knowledge of how it really feels to be addicted. He had to tackle Tyler's problems as an outsider, an unexperienced but loving father who was trying to save his child in the dark.

My mom and dad have similar parenting styles, both of relative fairness. My dad couldn't be defined as strict, but he certainly was not inattentive or carefree when it came to keeping us safe. He simply wanted to know where we were going and who we would be with—he did not monitor our location or demand an 8:00 p.m. curfew. We always had the freedom to have a full social life so long as we were communicative, safe, and made room for family time. We were also provided for financially and had resources available should we need them.

Nevertheless, what kind of parenting style do you adopt when you know your sixteen-year-old son has done meth? Medical or psychological intervention is certainly important, but how do you navigate your own relationship with an addicted child? With Tyler, everything changed. My dad couldn't just carry along with the same parenting or health teacher techniques that had worked well enough up until this point because Tyler was constantly untrustworthy and couldn't be counted on to even keep himself safe. While it would be foolish to let him come and go like the rest of us, it could also be equally dangerous if he tried to put Tyler on lockdown and caused him to resent us, generating a bad relationship that could alienate his high-risk child from the love and resources that were helping him survive.

Before things escalated and Tyler was entered into rehab, my dad tried various tricks to keep an eye on him without causing a fight. He threw out or locked up all the alcohol in the house, and one time he even unscrewed Tyler's bedroom door hinges so they would squeak loud enough to wake my dad if he tried sneaking out. He didn't want to breathalyze Tyler or remove his privacy altogether but knew he had to tighten the reins somehow. When things became more serious and it was clear that Tyler had a real problem, my parents opted to help rather than punish him.

My dad and mom poured an endless amount of time and money into Tyler's recovery process, never shying away from helping him even when they weren't sure how to straddle the line of helping without being overbearing and driving him away. He, my stepmom, my mom, and my stepdad communicated endlessly together, tackling every decision together as a team. My dad credits this co-parenting as the element that got him through such a hard time. Sometimes when things were too much for him to handle, he would ask my stepmom to step in and communicate with my mom, letting them be the biggest conduits of information. Their biggest contribution to Tyler's recovery was undoubtedly admittance to a recovery facility. My parents spent more on Tyler's recovery than they did on four years of my college tuition. My dad would drive six hours each way, twice a month, to visit Tyler the year and a half he was in rehab.

Navigating life after Tyler left his program was another challenge that my dad took in stride. The two still had a close relationship despite the elephant of trust, or lack thereof, in the room. My parents sporadically drug tested Tyler, which he didn't enjoy but also understood. It was an incredibly difficult balance, especially since Tyler was now an adult, about to go to college. Tyler made it very clear during his last few months in recovery that his primary motivation to stay clean was the promise of college in the fall. As a legal adult, he now could not be babied or put under careful watch all the time, and my parents had heard enough horror stories of addicted children running away and living on the streets instead of tolerating strict parents. They were constantly dancing between heavy surveillance and giving him the opportunity to earn trust and become an adult.

Since Tyler died, my dad struggles with wondering if he made the right choices. I don't believe that any singular decision on my parents' part was the make-or-break moment. Tyler struggled for years, and so many factors led to his death. I understand why my dad finds it hard not to feel guilty for being unable to keep the person you love most in the world alive. I have felt it myself, wondering how we couldn't even achieve the bare minimum for Tyler. The guilt I feel as a sister is likely only a fraction of what my dad feels as the parent and legal guardian for someone he just couldn't keep safe. No matter how out of his control Tyler's struggles truly were, every parent would like to think they are able to provide for and protect their family at all costs.

Another consideration is there were many moments along the journey that could have been the end for Tyler much sooner than nineteen years. Had my dad not caught him stealing pills in middle school, he could have overdosed at age fourteen. Had my parents not decided to put him into rehab when they did, he could have gotten killed at sixteen. We will never know the domino effect of our every action. What I do know is that everything my dad ever did for Tyler was motivated by the urge to, above all, keep him alive. While my dad indeed produced a child that had innate psychological troubles, this was completely out of his control, and he did everything in his power once Tyler was born to mitigate the hardship of these troubles. I do not pretend to know if the nature of Tyler's mental health problems was genetic or just a statistical fluke, but other than providing 50 percent of Tyler's DNA, my dad never knowingly contributed to Tyler's issues.

I finally asked him the question that had been on my mind for months: "How are you getting through it, though?"

His first answer was wrestling. Even though Tyler didn't stick with the sport, the wrestling community has wrapped its arms around our family in ways I will forever be thankful for. I have a vivid memory of sitting in the pew at Tyler's viewing, watching a stream of people float by and offer their condolences, many of whom I had seen on the side of a mat yelling at a high schooler to sprawl. The other high school coaches in the area, my dad's peers and rivals, came out en masse to offer us support, which gave me more comfort about my dad's grieving process than anything else I have yet seen. It was important for me to feel like my dad was being cared for not just by people who knew or loved Tyler, but by people who specifically knew and loved *him*. One coach I had grown up around even edited Tyler's funeral video montage for us, free of charge and on extremely short notice.

The distraction and sense of purpose that wrestling has provided in the aftermath of Tyler's death was similarly irreplaceable.

"I needed wrestling," my dad admitted to me. "It was the only way to keep my mind occupied."

His primary occupation is a health and PE teacher, and when Tyler died, all learning was online because of COVID-19. Imagine teaching physical education to hundreds of middle schoolers via Zoom for six months. By the time Tyler died, my dad was restless and exhausted by virtual learning without many social opportunities, and the chances of there being a wrestling season were bleak.

However, by some miracle, Loudoun County Public Schools allowed for a bastardized version of a wrestling season, and my dad was back in action. Three months after

Tyler's death, he was coaching again, getting out of the house, and moving around. He was open with his team about what had happened.

"The second week of practice, I sat them down and told them," he said. "I felt like they needed to know, and I used it as a learning lesson."

His team and fellow coaches were there for him when he needed them, and they offered a reprieve from sadness when he couldn't stand to dwell on it anymore. Even though wrestling wasn't for Tyler, its effects have embraced those he loved in ways I am sure he would be incredibly thankful for.

My dad's second answer was music. Our dad was an avid marching band competition attendee, would golf with Tyler on sunny days, and while Tyler's math skills were far beyond his abilities, the two achieved symbiosis while playing musical duets together. One of my favorite videos of Tyler is from a few years ago of him sitting at his keyboard playing Billy Joel's "Piano Man," my dad next to him accompanying with the harmonica. He was learning "Bohemian Rhapsody" when he died, excited to show off his new song to our dad.

They listened to the same music as well. While Tyler grew into a love of rap music that my dad never shared, a big part of him retained my dad's musical influence. No matter his age, he still harbored an appreciation for the country/classic rock combo that my dad was always playing. Tyler would be in his room blasting Eminem and then hop in my dad's truck and belt out "The Devil Went Down to Georgia" on the way to the grocery store. Since we lost Tyler, my dad has been hearing those songs of theirs everywhere. We all have our ways of keeping Tyler close, and he feels the most connected when one of their jam songs comes on in the car.

"I've heard 'Come Sail Away' on the radio and in stores more times since Tyler died than I ever have in my life," my dad noted, and indeed, I've heard the Styx classic come on while out in public with him several times. This sometimes-spooky phenomenon brings a smile to his face every time, a much fonder way of remembering Tyler than staring at his headstone. He orders the foods he and Tyler both loved whenever we go out and tells my litter brother, Hudson, stories of what his big brother was like when he was five years old. My dad takes both the small moments of similarity and the more common moments of radical difference and loves Tyler regardless of how much or little the two had in common.

Dad also credits us, his family, for helping him through. Of course, having family members around is comforting, but it goes much deeper than that. My stepmom, Lindsey, lost her sister, my Aunt LaLa, in April of 2020, and going through that together made us all stronger and closer by the time we lost Tyler. Lindsey's parents, who we kids call Maw and Papa, are also some of the most faithful people my dad and I have ever met—their immovable trust in God's plan and the fact that LaLa and Tyler are together in heaven has been an enormous inspiration for the rest of us. Hudson also looks and acts just like Tyler, ever curious and obsessed with *Star Wars*. Tyler and LaLa were his favorite people, and he never lets us forget them. My dad's family network is solid, lifting him up whenever he needs it.

I can see it in my dad's face now and then, this pain in his eyes that's hard for me to stomach. It's even difficult for me to look at him sometimes; he and Tyler look so much alike. While traces of my mom are sometimes claimed in our faces, my dad and Tyler are carbon copies of one another—I would challenge anyone to tell their baby pictures apart. My dad sympathized with Tyler's lack of emotional vulnerability, seeing his own quiet contemplation mirrored in the way that Tyler used humor and fun to distract from what he was really feeling. Despite his best efforts, my dad lost a huge part of himself.

I saw how my dad agonized over Tyler while he was alive, trying everything he could think of to prevent the outcome that happened, and I can see how badly he is hurting now. He isn't very vocal, but I know my dad misses his conundrum of a child who ended up being the best companion he could have asked for. He's grieving in his own way, using his support network, and trying to remain grateful for the good parts as best as he can. I just hope that over time the pain subsides and is replaced with happy memories, and my dad can move away from blaming himself for Tyler's loss and cherish the beautiful moments playing music with his little space alien with a heart of gold.

IV

Our "nuclear family," as Tyler and I knew it, did not officially form until my dad and mom remarried in 2010 and 2011. Our parents split up when I was eleven, Tyler seven, and each recoupled within three years of the divorce. Tyler and I were both old enough to remember the time before the separation, but still young enough that our essential years were spent growing up alongside these new family members. Those who know our family today know it is a large conglomeration of halves, wholes, and steps. It might seem complicated to an outsider, but I want to make something very clear: our giant, confusing family is a happy one.

As I begin the work of explaining how and why Tyler abused substances, I must address a common perception of divorce and blended families as a stressful or traumatizing factor in a child's life. During the many years when Tyler was struggling, there were a lot of questions both from medical and personal supporters about how our family situation might be affecting Tyler's mental state or causing him to want to take drugs.

Simply put, an entire body of research is dedicated to predicting the effects of divorce on a child's likelihood to use drugs. Famously, David Sheff spends the first two chapters of his memoir, *Beautiful Boy,* theorizing the reasons for his son's addiction. He keeps circling back to the influence of his divorce on Nic, his young child. He partially blames his own failed relationship as a trigger for Nic's later methamphetamine abuse (Sheff, 2008). In his own version of events, Nic himself states, "Children seem like empty vessels who pick up on everything and are so affected by their surroundings" (Sheff, 2008).

While I do believe the divorce certainly changed our lives, I don't think it did so negatively, and I feel strongly that our family structure was not a cause for Tyler's addiction. The American Society for the Positive Care of Children has identified a list of adverse childhood events (ACEs) that, if occurring to a child under the age of eighteen, can have potentially lifelong ramifications like risky health behaviors, early death, low life potential, or chronic health conditions. These events include traumatic occurrences like physical abuse or neglect. Notably, however, they do not include divorce. A parents' disappearance from a child's life is considered an ACE, but an amicable split is not. (American Society for the Positive Care of Children, 2021).

A study on family instability by Dr. Paula Fomby and Dr. Andrew J. Cherlin also concludes:

> *"Children who experience multiple transitions in family structure may fare worse developmentally than children raised in stable two-parent families and perhaps even than children raised in stable, single-parent families. However, multiple transitions and negative child outcomes may be associated because of common causal factors such as parents' antecedent behaviors and attributes."*
>
> (FOMBY AND CHERLIN, 2007).

Basically, the research shows that in cases of children suffering post-divorce, the trauma was usually a result of the parents' prior characteristics and behaviors rather than the shift in the family dynamic itself. Luckily for Tyler and me, our parents had the most cordial divorce I have ever heard of, and neither are abusive or absent. To this day, my parents still live roughly two miles down the road from each other. While Tyler and I were still in grade school, they took co-parenting seriously, both showing up to our music or sporting events and never making it awkward to be in the same room together. They made Tyler's and my happiness their first priority, minimizing the adverse effects of this new lifestyle. To be honest, since we were reassured that we would still get to see both parents, the rest didn't matter. What I remember as the worst part about the actual breakup was arguing with Tyler over who got the bigger room in dad's new townhouse. This was immediately pacified by a shopping trip to Target where we picked out a second set of pajamas and toothbrushes. At our young ages, the status of our parents' romantic relationship was simply immaterial. In fact, the more Christmases, the merrier.

Even after Tyler and I both turned eighteen, we still rotated holidays as per the custody agreement of our childhood. Before his death, my parents still communicated virtually every day because Tyler still needed quite a bit of parenting. Especially when COVID-19 hit in early 2020 and Tyler was living back home, there was always a schedule to be coordinated or a suspicion of relapse to be discussed. Over the years, I saw their co-parenthood turn into a mutual respect and friendship. The two of them were high school sweethearts from the same small Midwest town and share four decades of history. My dad still goes on vacation with my mom's dad and uncle. Sometimes my grandpa and great-uncle will still come to Virginia for a few days to play in my dad's annual pool tournament, maybe stopping by to see my mom, their daughter/niece, on the way out of town. My mom and Lindsey text each other instead of communicating through my dad—he is awful at texting, and the two of them are much better at planning anyway.

I do not want to claim that divorce is not inherently traumatizing and disregard the lived experiences of others who are not as lucky as Tyler and I were. Everyone's situation is different, and our mom and dad took great pains to achieve an unusually peaceful separation. I am speaking from my unique perspective and using research to dispute the notion that my family situation was a factor in Tyler's rocky life trajectory and eventual premature death. There is an infinite number of reasons why people become addicted to illicit substances, and while many of them involve family stressors, I want everyone who reads Tyler's story to know that he never once blamed our parents' decisions and loved the new additions to our family as much as the originals.

The truth of the matter is that my parents were not happy together, and they did what they thought was the best for everyone, most importantly the kids. I personally believe that we were better off with divorced, happy parents than married, miserable ones. What if they stayed together, and I never had a model for what a healthy marriage looks like? So, no, I never heard Tyler speak a single resentment toward our parents for getting divorced, nor did he ever allude to it ruining his life or turn him down a dark path toward addiction.

As I mentioned earlier, Tyler was a hyperactive child almost from birth. When asked why he uses drugs, his reason is always a version of, "I can't turn my brain off." His constantly racing mind was evident long before the first sign of our parents' marital strife. The National Institute on Drug Abuse cites a 2020 family study that suggests a person's genetic makeup alone accounts for up to half of their risk factor for addiction.

The only notable problems that occurred were growing pains starting when our mom and dad got into new relationships. They both started dating their current spouses almost immediately after they split up, and that was exponentially more challenging for us both to deal with than Mommy and Daddy living in two separate houses. Both my mom's new boyfriend, Jeff, and my dad's new girlfriend, Lindsey, had a combined five children from previous relationships, so more jarring than my family splitting up was the sudden addition of seven new members.

My stepmother, Lindsey, was a particularly difficult relationship to navigate. She was my dad's coworker, teaching middle school physical education with him. The two had been friends since before my parents divorced, so I already knew her, albeit in a different light. While she was fourteen years younger than he was, she had two children, Courtney and Connor, in the same grades as Tyler and me, respectively. While Courtney and Tyler quickly became playmates in that easy way that seven-year-olds do, Connor, the cool guy at his school, did not have much in common with a girl in a goth phase with most of her friend group in band class. Lindsey, too, presented more of a challenge for adolescent Alexis than she did for Tyler.

Since the classic fairy tale *Cinderella* of the seventeenth century, the image of the evil stepmother has pervaded literature and popular media. As a middle school girl trying to navigate teenage angst and puberty with the body of a green bean, I had no patience for this new pseudo-mother figure in my life. Now that I am older and love my stepmom to death, I can reflect more clearly on why she was a particular source of anger for me and understand that our conflict was twofold: we have very similar personalities (we even look alike—we both have blonde curls, while my mom's hair is stick straight and Lindsey's daughter, Courtney's, is brown), and we were constantly competing to be "right," especially in the eyes of my dad. Every showdown seemed to be a battle of two similar minds, with my dad as the judge. One of us would do something to enrage the other, war would ensue, and my dad would be stuck in the middle. Each time my dad lectured me or told me I was in the wrong, I felt that I was not only losing the fight but also losing my dad as well.

Tyler never seemed to be as bothered by Lindsey as I was. Sure, there were times when we would hide in a pillow fort, complaining about how annoying she was, but it was really me who struggled the most with the new family dynamics. Maybe it was because Tyler was so young that, by the time he was old enough to be capable of real interpersonal conflict, Lindsey and Jeff were already firmly positioned as parts of our family, no longer newcomers. If he had any personality conflicts like I did with Lindsey, they were less serious. To him, Jeff and Lindsey had already been there when he reached the teenage angst phase. He did not experience them as new invaders, the way I had. Going through something as a child is not the same as and going through it as a preteen, and I think that was the key difference in how Tyler and I handled the divorce. I theoretically had it worse than Tyler did, but even my issues did not qualify as an ACE.

In fact, Tyler was mostly the one supporting me through it all. I remember one particularly nasty incident, at a beach house with Lindsey's extended family on my sixteenth birthday. It involved an argument and a thrown drink and ended with me calling her a bitch in front of forty of our closest relatives and loved ones.

I sprinted down the beach house stairs and threw open the door to the movie room, where Tyler, like he did on most days at the beach, was avoiding the sand and sun in favor of darkness and a screen.

"We gotta go!" I shouted, tossing his Sperrys at him.

Without a word, he put them on and ran after me, out the front door, down the driveway, and north along the beach road. Once we were out of earshot of the house, we finally broke down in hysterical laughter. He was laughing at my frenzied, inexplicable behavior, I at his unquestioning sense of urgency. He tore out of the house with me without a single clue as to why we were running. We were a quarter mile away before I finally caught my breath enough to tell him what happened. From that sense of knowing that only siblings have, he understood that I needed him, and was there for me, no questions asked.

Tyler and Lindsey butted heads much less often, if ever. Tyler was one of the most laid-back people I knew, rarely complaining or willingly starting conflict. Lindsey is also the most maternal person I've ever met—she always says that if she could have ten children, she would. Lindsey saw Tyler's sweet nature as a gift, and truly felt like she gained two more children through my dad, regardless of blood. As we got older, Tyler and I both learned to really love Lindsey, and appreciate the heart of gold under the exterior we sometimes clashed with. I think we all matured and really became a blended family, learning to navigate each other's many personality traits, good and bad.

Moments with Lindsey in the years while I was in college and Tyler in high school mostly involved her being a great stepmom and friend to us both. She dragged my dad and siblings to watch me play various instruments in marching band, from home football games to the Macy's Thanksgiving Day Parade. For Tyler, she organized a fun Thanksgiving trip in New England so he could attend, even while still in his recovery program. The two of them had their own inside jokes, especially about food—Lindsey was always bringing him caramel cream cold brew from Starbucks or a Taco Bell Doritos Locos Taco. She tried to sneak him the energy drinks he wanted after my dad had banned them. Whenever she went to Costco, he'd never turn down the chance to ask for some goodies, even if he was days away from leaving for college. She treats us both like her own blood, and I know she'd do anything for us. I couldn't pinpoint a moment when Tyler and I started to love and appreciate my stepmom, but my memories of us arguing in my youth seem funny to me now, incompatible with our current relationship.

The running family joke is that Lindsey is the person to call if you ever needed to buy a house, got pregnant, or were in jail. Along with her health and PE teacher job, she is also a licensed realtor and pediatric registered nurse. With her medical expertise, she was the one who recommended Tyler get allergy shots so he could get the cat he wanted and not be miserable. His whole life, Tyler had to take an assortment of medications, and Lindsey was able to bond with him, the only one in the family who knew about what he was actually taking. Their bond grew when our half-brother, Hudson, was born because Tyler quickly became his hero. The two were inseparable, and this new connection enhanced all those around it.

In the past year, I have learned even more about my step-mom's admirable qualities, including a strength I had previously never witnessed at this magnitude. Less than four months before Tyler passed, Lindsey's sister Lisa died. In her mid-fifties, my Aunt LaLa was everyone's favorite fun aunt. She had no children of her own, so she poured herself into her nieces and nephews, coming to our big events, sending us a card for every occasion, getting us the most thoughtful Christmas gifts. She was that person who livened up every room she entered, loud and full of joy. Her entire apartment's worth of belongings was still in our front room waiting to be sorted when my mom called Dad and Lindsey to tell them that Tyler was gone. Her funeral, which was supposed to be my first, ended up being one week after Tyler's. He was slated to play "Hallelujah" on the piano at her service.

Lindsey was right in the epicenter of LaLa's and Tyler's deaths. Many people knew and therefore had to mourn both, but a sister and stepson were two particularly close relationships to lose at once. She was already in the middle of the worst loss of her life, and suddenly that had competition.

Then she called me around 2:00 a.m. the morning of Tyler's funeral.

"Can you come to the vet? We have to put Heidi down."

I hung up the phone and began laughing uncontrollably. No, this could not be real. Our eleven-year-old golden retriever, Heidi, who had been playing and running around hours before, was internally bleeding on an emergency veterinarian table. *The day of Tyler's funeral.*

I sped over and climbed in the truck with my dad, Lindsey, and stepsister Courtney. The four of us were stunned, unable to process the reality of what was happening. When the vet was finally ready for us, she told us the following:

"Heidi has an abscess in her abdomen that has ruptured and is bleeding internally. We don't know if it's malignant, but this is very common in golden retrievers. It would cost $750 to stabilize her, and then more depending on how extensive the surgery will be. She might live another week, maybe more, it's hard to tell. It's totally up to you guys if you—"

"Can we get this over with?" Lindsey interrupted her. "We have to bury our son in six hours."

The vet blinked at her, clearly thinking she misheard. Was this some kind of sick joke?

We ended up putting Heidi down that night, as an attempt at saving her would be expensive, and ultimately prolong her suffering without offering more than a few weeks' time. My dad waited in the lobby, unable to watch. Courtney, Lindsey, and I followed the vet into the back room where Heidi lay, panting heavily, on a sterile table, tubes sticking out of her every which way.

"Say hi to Tyler for me," I whispered at 3:00 a.m. the day of my brother's funeral, clutching Lindsey's arm with one hand, stroking Heidi's paw with the other, as the vet injected phenobarbital into her IV. I felt her body relax and watched her eyes gloss over, knowing her spirit was on its way to Tyler.

That incident, and Lindsey's subsequent actions, taught me one of the biggest lessons about grief that no one prepares you for: life continues. Just because your world stops, does not mean everyone else's does. Time persists, dogs age, bills must be paid, deadlines must be met, other tragedies happen. You are not spared by the universe because you are suffering, nor can you remove yourself from the passage of time to fully immerse yourself in grief.

Lindsey gave my dad's speech for him at Tyler's funeral when he couldn't. She arranged Heidi's cremation and got us all paw print mementos. A week later, she attended her sister's funeral, where she gave another speech and comforted her parents and brother. Then, after the chaos subsided, she went back to work. She is somehow juggling her own grief with taking care of my dad and five-year-old brother, selling houses, teaching middle school health and PE full time, working as an on-call pediatric registered nurse, and getting a second master's degree. She is the one getting my dad and Hudson out of bed every morning while fulfilling her duties in four occupations. I can't make this up—my stepmom can and does do it all.

This is not to say that she doesn't have her own difficult moments. Sometimes I wonder how she can stand to pinball back and forth between mourning two of the most important people in her life and watching others mourn around her. Instead of wallowing and letting things crumble around her, she has planned fun weekend getaways for us, gotten a new puppy, and is working on signing everyone in the family up for counseling. While our relationship was already in a close and loving place before Tyler died, her strength and commitment to keeping my family and herself living and moving forward has given me an elevated respect for her.

This is why, when I read these accounts of awful divorces that have lasting ramifications on the children, I simply cannot relate to them. I'm sure that 99 percent of divorces are worse than my parents' was, and that some kids have indeed done drugs to cope with the pain of their home dissolving. Regardless, for Tyler and me, our parents' divorce and remarriages were a net gain. After some initial bumps, we really did nothing but gain a bigger support network. I know Tyler was grateful for his stepmom, and I know how thankful I am to have her helping me through my own pain. She happens to now be one of my closest confidantes, and the two of us are only making it through because of the love we share for her sister, my baby brother, and each other.

V

———

People underestimate the manic episode that is planning a funeral. Dying is so logistically complicated, especially when the deceased is only nineteen years old, with nothing death-related prepared. We had to pick out a plot, a casket, his outfit, write an obituary, plan a schedule, reserve locations, call a caterer for the celebration of life, decide between embalmment versus cremation, order death certificates, rent transportation, coordinate with not one, but two pastors, print programs, write speeches, choose songs, create a video montage...I could go on. It was, in a word, exhausting. I credit this overwhelming organization for leaving me completely numb the day of the funeral. I gave a full speech at Tyler's funeral without even tearing up.

After the funeral, when we all finally let ourselves crumble, it was my stepdad Jeff who took over the logistical flurry. I was in a predicament, unsure of when was the appropriate time to go back to Los Angeles, where I was living at the time. I decided on returning after two months, and I was nervous about leaving my mom on the other end of the country from her only remaining child. I have since moved back home to be closer to her between the first holiday season and leaving for graduate school, but at the time, Jeff was the only reason

I felt comfortable going back to LA at all. I knew he would be taking care of my mom in my absence when I couldn't fathom the idea of her left alone with one child dead, the other across the country. Jeff reassured me that he would take care of her. And he did.

For instance, headstones take months to arrive. Before Tyler's was installed, all that marked his grave (besides flowers and trinkets from family and friends) was a tiny plastic marker with his name and dates inscribed on it. Jeff found a website that specializes in miniature granite engravings, and he had a small mock-up of the headstone rush ordered to the house and surprised my mom with it the week after I left. She called me in tears, which was not uncommon, but for the first time in weeks, they were tears of joy. This intrinsic thoughtfulness is the only reason I am able to sleep at night and am not consumed with worry for my mom. Jeff, while he cannot truly understand what my mom is going through, *does* understand what she needs. Whether you believe in soulmates or not, he has a fundamental knowledge of how to support my mom that I can only describe as rare.

Jeff's goal, since the moment it became clear we were going to be a blended family, was to integrate as seamlessly as possible. Often when I talk about my family, I refer to my stepparents or stepsiblings as simply my parents or siblings, casting off the "step-" prefix out of laziness or love, sometimes both. There are many times where the line is blurred, and we are really one big family, but it would be naive to pretend that there are not differences between biological family and family by marriage. Especially since both my dad and Jeff's ex-wife are still alive and present, the stepparent plays a role moored in parental purgatory.

As long as I've known him, Jeff has carefully attempted to both act as father figure to Tyler and me while not stepping on the toes of our father. In high school I would call him my "vice-dad," and while it's goofy, that's truly what he is. As far as parenting goes, he is more an extension of my mom's authority than of a dad, and as far as affection goes, he loves me and Tyler deeply, yet in a different way than he loves his own children.

Just like Lindsey at Costco, Jeff always catered to Tyler's extensive and often silly food requests at the grocery store. He would come home with a bag full of Slim Jims and Dr. Pepper, just because it made Tyler happy. He also attended our events and milestone moments, showing up to a Virginia basketball game or Tyler's high school marching band competition, wearing the respective school colors. He never griped about the cost or inconvenience of Tyler being in a recovery program. When my mom wanted to be with her son on Christmas, Jeff brought the rest of the family along so we could all be together, and even researched fun restaurants and things to do in the area of his recovery facility.

Jeff's relationship with Tyler was especially hard to navigate as Tyler required a *lot* of parenting. Every time Tyler got in trouble, put himself in danger, or otherwise stressed my mom out, Jeff could only offer advice, but he never had the final word. It often felt like they were going in circles without an obvious solution. Let's pretend Tyler got caught sneaking alcohol. The conversation would have gone something like this:

Mom: "I think I should ground him for a month, what do you think?"

Jeff: "He keeps doing this, you just take his phone and ground him for a month. He's not learning anything from this."

Mom: "I just don't know what to do anymore."

Jeff: "I mean, we've grounded him for a month so many times and it hasn't made him stop. I feel like we need to focus on something other than discipline if we're going to get through to him."

Mom: "I know, I just don't know what that other thing is."

Jeff: "…Okay."

After Tyler passed, he told me how he felt as if he was too hard on Tyler sometimes, and wondered if he totally screwed up the vice-parent role. I knew this was ridiculous, and Tyler would have laughed at this too. Jeff is not perfect, yet his good intentions to co-raise Tyler and me were perfectly clear.

Imagine the position Jeff is in. His partner has two children from a previous marriage who are not his own but must be considered in all things. He could easily have chosen a hands-off approach or resented Tyler. He never made my mom choose between him and Tyler, gave an ultimatum or kicked him out of the house. He considered Tyler's needs as a child the same way he considered his own children's needs. Every issue Tyler was having were not just my mom's problems, but Jeff's too. He stepped up as a parent, offering his own expertise and opinions while deferring to my mom for ultimate authority. I commend him for this approach, as I have witnessed other friends with divorced parents who have not had this experience. Jeff's commitment to operating as a family unit was always apparent to Tyler and me both, even if we did not always like having another voice of authority.

It's simply weird to let new people enter your lives and live in your home with you. While we are a fully integrated family now, at one point, Jeff, Lindsey, and their kids were complete strangers to Tyler and me. I take for granted how good we have it, the symbiosis we have achieved that is certainly not a universal result of remarriages. I think of how much we've been through, the events that have solidified us as a family in place of blood ties. Since I met Jeff and Lindsey as an awkward sixth-grader, and Tyler as a second-grader, we have watched Jeff lose a father and stop eating gluten for his own health reasons, and Lindsey lose her sister and struggle with multiple sclerosis (MS). Tyler would ask Lindsey about the sodium levels in different foods after she had to adopt a more MS-friendly diet, while I found special gluten-free treats for Jeff's birthdays. In turn, they have supported us for now over a decade, comforting us after breakups, driving us to sports practices, and cheering for us as we walked across various graduation stages.

These are the moments that matter, the moments that earn you a spot on the family roster. These moments are the reason I proudly tell people I have seven siblings and four parents, despite the follow-up work I always have to do ("No, we are not Mormon"). I remember the day of Tyler's funeral before the viewing started, one of the rare moments when all four parents and eight children were together in the same room. I remember looking around, thinking there was no one else I'd rather see here than the people who became my family in an unconventional way. I find the most love and comfort in these people who *chose* to be my family, to love my mom or dad and me and Tyler more than the baggage they came with.

The biggest way that Jeff helped Tyler, and by extension the rest of our family, was by helping to figure out a plan for Tyler's recovery. While he and my mom did not always agree on the best way to punish bad behavior, they needed to be 100 percent in agreement about the enormous financial decision that was sending Tyler to a rehab facility.

Addiction treatment can be extremely difficult to access for a variety of reasons. A 2016 study showed that only about 18 percent of those who needed addiction treatment actually received any, mostly because of problems like program availability, stigma, co-occurring disorders, or cost. Since addiction has long been treated as a social or criminal issue rather than a health care one, demand for addiction treatment far outweighs the supply of treatment options available (American Addiction Centers, 2016). Famously, David Sheff recalls the absurd number of phone calls he had to make in order to find a bed for Nic in a recovery facility, knowing that if he continued to be turned down, Nic would end up on the street (Sheff, 2008).

Some addiction treatment facilities require a patient to be sober when they enter, an insurmountable feat for many. Others do not allow the use or prescription of Suboxone (buprenorphine) or methadone, a medication many opioid addicts rely on to curb the side effects of opioid withdrawal, because of its abusable properties, government restrictions, and stigma against medicinal addiction treatment (Rapaport, 2020).

In Tyler's case, the biggest barrier to treatment was cost. While most medical insurance companies theoretically cover addiction treatment, there is always a battle about what is "needed." My mom recalled to me a frustrating conversation with an insurance agent shortly before they denied coverage for his recovery completely.

"We just don't think Tyler needs live-in treatment," she told my mom.

"You mean...the kid who was just deemed passively suicidal from a team of licensed psychiatrists?" my mom was stunned.

Tyler had to move from a facility in California to one on the East Coast when insurance stopped paying, and my mom and Jeff had to figure out a way to pay for his treatment completely out of pocket. Jeff and my mom make good money but paying tens of thousands of dollars unexpectedly was not easy. Jeff dealt with the financial planner and stayed strong for my mom, reassuring her that this was absolutely necessary, that their child was in danger, and they would go to any lengths to save him.

Tyler was extremely lucky in this sense since for most people, that kind of money is simply not accessible. What about people with no insurance, or people who can't afford to relocate out of state because no beds are available in their own geographic location? I can't help but think about how insanely difficult Tyler's recovery facility journey was, even though he had more financial advantages than most. Across the country, most people in our predicament do not end up receiving any addiction treatment and are forced to face their battle without health care.

I always commended Jeff for jumping in without question, never begrudging Tyler for being so expensive, and for offering him the same resources he would his own children. He made sure that we always felt like a united front so Tyler would never feel guilty for taking advantage of their means. Tyler and I were objectively lucky, and I will always keep that in my heart when I think about all we did to save him.

Another moment of thankfulness I felt after losing Tyler was when Jeff picked me up from the airport the day Tyler died. It was upon seeing him that I realized Tyler was truly gone. All day I had been in a daze, making travel plans and trying to understand what was happening, but silently hoping that maybe it wasn't actually true. I had barely spoken to my mom after her initial phone call, so a small piece of me wondered if maybe she was just being hysterical, maybe he was in a coma, maybe when Jeff picked me up, we would rush to the hospital. I expected Jeff to be frustrated, annoyed at Tyler for scaring us yet again, and putting mom in so much distress.

When I walked out the sliding doors of the airport, Jeff's shoulders were slumped, and he was crying. He hugged me with a love and protectiveness I have never felt before, and we wept together.

"I'm sorry," was all he managed to say.

His expression had nothing to do with regard for my mom's feelings, but everything to do with the fact that there was nothing left to be done, and Jeff was now suffering an insurmountable loss himself. Standing outside of Dulles International, I realized that it was really, truly over. Here was my tough, strong stepdad holding me and sobbing with me over the person I love most in the world. That doesn't just happen—that is the result of years of togetherness and dedication to our family. Not that I ever questioned Jeff's loyalty or love for us, yet sometimes it takes these dark moments to remind you just how real it is.

Especially when you get older, you start to develop a relationship with your step-people that just comes from your true compatibility. I love Jeff and Lindsey because my parents love them, sure, but I also love Jeff because he tells me what to do when a light comes on in my dashboard, and Lindsey because she gives the best Christmas gifts ever. I imagine being a stepparent to be one of the most difficult things you could ever be to someone, juggling your romantic relationship with a pseudo-parental role with the feelings of your own children.

Tyler and I were extraordinarily lucky to have stepparents we get along with. I never wish that my parents were still married, and Tyler didn't either. Now especially, I can't imagine how the two of them would survive this loss if they were still married to each other; I think their combined grief would fester and they would not be able to help each other. Now, they both have a strong partner to support them in their grief, and three extra children apiece to live for.

I am forever grateful for my broken, blended, perfect family, and Tyler was too.

VI

Our five-year-old half-brother, Hudson, presents one of the trickiest dynamics of Tyler's death. How do you explain death to someone that young so that they understand but aren't traumatized? Child psychologists say that preschool-aged children sometimes struggle with the finality of death, not quite grasping that the person is physically gone forever (Salek and Ginsburg, 2014). I was startled by how fully Hudson seems to comprehend how permanent death is, but it didn't start with Tyler.

In April 2020, just four months before Tyler died, Hudson experienced his first family death, our Aunt Lisa (my stepmom Lindsey's sister). Hudson knew her as his Aunt LaLa, who would drive up from Richmond to surprise him at preschool, dress up in intricate costumes for her job as a haunted house performer, and bring him the coolest birthday and Christmas gifts. She truly encapsulated the archetype of the fun aunt—with no children of her own, she poured all her love and energy into us, her incredibly lucky nieces and nephews. Much like Tyler, she possessed a knack for entertaining and an energy that never seemed to wane.

Lisa was one of those people whose presence was made known as soon as she entered the room. At five feet nine inches with a mane of huge, blonde curls, she would catch your attention even if she was completely silent. However, her voice carried, and she was always laughing—sometimes you heard her before you even saw her. She attended every one of our events, from birthday parties to marching band performances to piano recitals. Any five-year-old would have adored her big smile and bright persona, and Hudson was no exception.

Lisa and Tyler were also similar in that they were Hudson's favorites, the only two who could sit and genuinely listen to whatever he had to say, even if it was a thirty-minute, unintelligible rant about *Star Wars*. They engaged when others would nod or ignore him entirely. While LaLa's brother and father suffered from heart conditions, she was considered the healthy one of the family. Always doing yoga and advocating for healthy living, Lisa took physical and mental well-being extremely seriously.

The issue of explaining death to Hudson first arose in the aftermath of a shocking phone call my stepmom received after not hearing from Lisa for a few days. Her dad called her, worried, and the two of them checked to see if she had posted on Facebook or contacted any of her friends. Their efforts showed no sign of her. It was also their brother Dow's birthday, and Lisa missed it entirely. This was so out of character that her dad requested the police do a wellness check. After forcibly entering the apartment where she lived alone, police found her dead. Dow called Lindsey in a fashion very similar to my mom's call to me a few months later, to relay the absolute worst-case scenario.

Hudson handled the news well, all things considered. My dad and Lindsey, in the midst of their own grief, told him that LaLa was gone. My family is also very faithful and raised

Hudson to believe in God, so they softened the blow of finality with an emphasis on heaven, explaining that Lisa was at peace, invisible but still watching over him. They explained to him that everybody dies when they get older and tried to quell his fears by assuring him that he wouldn't die for a very long time. They attempted to help him process the natural sequence of events, saying that one day, his grandparents would also go to heaven. He appeared to be genuinely sad and seemed to understand that while she was gone, it was the natural way of things. He mostly seemed to focus on the fact that Lisa was *gone*. She was cremated, so he never saw her lifeless body, but he understood that he would not spend time with her or talk to her again. Hudson is a smart kid, and we were relieved that he had a healthy grasp of such a hard topic.

How, then, do you explain to Hudson that his nineteen-year-old brother has also suddenly died? Death seemed to make sense to him when it followed the natural order of things, the inevitable finale to a long and fulfilling life. How do you make him understand the unlikeliness of it, the horror and unnatural nuances of losing a person that young?

Lindsey immediately took Hudson to our neighbors' house when my dad received the Tyler phone call. She didn't know what was going to happen, but that it probably wouldn't be suitable for a five-year-old to watch. He stayed there for the rest of the day and even spent the night, but he knew something was wrong. When Lindsey picked him up the next day, his little face was intensely worried. My dad and Lindsey immediately sat him down on the back porch and said they had to tell him something.

"Buddy...Tyler died."

"What?" He screwed up his little nose in confusion. "Are you serious?"

My dad and Lindsey immediately jumped in with platitudes and reassurances.

"He's with LaLa in heaven now," Lindsey told him, holding back her own tears.

"I wish he just had a broken leg," Hudson was starting to cry now. "I wish he was just in the hospital."

He then started to scream, just as all of us adults had.

A few days after this episode, Lindsey's parents drove up from Virginia Beach for the funeral. Maw and Papa, who so recently lost their own daughter, have been an anchor to both my parents and Hudson alike. They are also some of Hudson's favorite people, yet upon seeing them that day, Hudson angrily demanded of my grandpa, "Why are you still alive but Tyler's dead? I didn't want Tyler to die!"

These questions and outbursts were a common theme those first few weeks as Hudson came to terms with his new reality. The day after Tyler's death, my dad and Lindsey brought him to my mom and Jeff's house, where we all gathered to figure out what the hell to do. As soon as he saw me, Hudson immediately asked me what time Tyler had died. When I told him sometime in the middle of the night, he made a face of deep consideration and walked off. He later asked my mom if he could still come over and swim in her pool, even though Tyler wasn't there to take him. His mind was churning, thinking through all the ramifications of what it means to lose your brother in the hyper-logical way only a child can. I couldn't help but look at this little guy thinking away, sad but grateful that in only five short years, he had formed such a strong connection with his big brother.

Hudson joined the family in 2015, when I was a senior in high school. I was unhappy about the pregnancy announcement at first. It infuriated me, actually. I didn't like the idea of my dad having another child that wasn't me or Tyler, with a woman that wasn't my mom. I was also not keen on the fact that he was already fifty-one years old. What I didn't predict was how much I would love Hudson. He was not just my dad's new kid, but my and Tyler's baby brother. And holy crap, was he cute. You know how some babies are just straight up ugly, but you're supposed to say that all babies are cute? Hudson was *gorgeous*. People would always comment on how cute he was, even as a newborn. Now that he's five, his inquisitive, charming personality makes him even more adorable. An old friend of mine, after playing forty-five minutes of rock-paper-scissors with Hudson, remarked, "This kid should be on Disney Channel."

Tyler never had an issue with the idea of a new baby, though. In fact, when Lindsey and Dad first told us they were going to have a baby, eighth-grade Tyler's only question was, "Is it gonna be a guy or a girl?" This question was so funny to us that when we later found out the baby's sex, Lindsey exclaimed, "Congratulations, it's a guy!"

Tyler and I adored Hudson immediately, although neither of us had a particularly strong parental instinct. My favorite memory of my two brothers happened during the first time my dad and Lindsey asked Tyler and I to babysit for a few hours. Hudson was still an infant, and things were going fine until it became apparent that he had pooped. Neither Tyler nor I had ever changed a diaper before, so we consulted YouTube and tried calling our parents until I ultimately told Tyler to just do it already and left the room like the mature sister I am. Five minutes later, he emerged looking triumphant, but he was still holding a screaming baby.

"Why is he still upset?" I asked, panicking.

"I don't know! I changed the diaper!" Tyler looked bewildered and handed Hudson to me.

"Maybe you put it on wrong?" I decided to inspect his handiwork and laid Hudson back onto the changing table to undo the fresh diaper.

I immediately saw the problem. While Tyler had indeed changed the diaper correctly, he neglected to clean Hudson off at all. Hudson was still completely covered in poop.

"*Tyler*," I tried to sound condescending, but I was in tears of laughter. I had minimal knowledge of babies, but even I knew you had to at least clean the poop off a baby before you put on a new diaper. I wiped Hudson using approximately forty baby wipes, he finally stopped crying, and our parents never let us babysit again.

It pained me and my older stepbrother, Connor, to leave for college right when our new brother was born, while Tyler and my stepsister Courtney got to have four years living in the same house as Hudson while they were in high school (technically two and a half years for Tyler, since he left for rehab his junior year of high school). Whenever we ask him, Hudson is sweet enough to say he loves all his siblings equally, yet we know he has a soft spot for Tyler. Even when Tyler was in rehab, the journeys to visit him in California or Connecticut were fun trips to toddler-aged Hudson. Nerf guns, Legos, and lightsaber fights filled their days, and Tyler had an inimitable ability to keep up with the little ball of energy, perhaps because his own brain was on full speed at all times. When he hit the toddler stage, Hudson's incessant questions never phased Tyler; instead, he took them seriously and answered him with a respect and patience I surely do not possess.

Hudson was heartbroken when Tyler and Courtney went off to college themselves. He was now the only child living at home with siblings in four different states, the closest four hours away. Even though he came to many of my college's football games and road-tripped to move Courtney into her freshman dorm at the University of Kentucky, he still thought of college as an evil, sibling-snatching monster. He was elated when COVID-19 happened because his big brother Tyler got to come home and spend virtually every day with him from March until August 2020. They had just gone on a road trip to Kentucky and Illinois together, and Hudson was becoming used to having his big brother around full time. With this in mind, it is no surprise that after Tyler's death, Hudson once looked at me with tears in his eyes and said, "It's like Tyler's in college forever."

Then the day of the funeral came. Until then, I think Hudson was doing a good job of understanding the permanence of death because he could not see Tyler. Whether Tyler was in college or dead, it didn't matter—to Hudson, he was gone. Except...how does a five-year-old hold on to this sense of loss when the body of their loved one is lying right in front of him?

Our family filed into the viewing room of the funeral chapel, some of us wailing, some of us crumpling to the floor. Hudson was sitting on my lap, completely silent, just staring at the visible top half of Tyler's embalmed body in its casket. It looked like Tyler, it wore one of Tyler's Hawaiian shirts, but it didn't smile or play lightsabers like Tyler. Its eyes didn't light up and it didn't spread its arms out for a big spinning hug like Tyler. Hudson was morbidly quiet, clinging to my arm and just staring at what was left of his brother, who was supposed to be gone but was somehow right in front of him.

Then his little face grew panicked, and he whispered, "Alexis, where are Tyler's legs?"

I set him on the ground and ran out of the chapel into the bathroom, collapsing on the tile and retching while my uncle's girlfriend, who happened to be washing her hands when I barged in, held me. Hudson couldn't see Tyler's legs under the closed half of the casket, so he wasn't sure they were still there. It made me so sad to wonder what Hudson was imagining, thinking Tyler's body to be legless, having no knowledge of funeral rituals or what happens to the body after you die.

Before we closed the casket, Hudson nestled a lightsaber in next to Tyler, telling us, "What if he needs it?" At the gravesite, he plastered the casket with Lego *Star Wars* stickers while the pastor said the final prayer and demanded that we stay to watch them lower Tyler into the ground. While this was not part of the normal funeral procedure, we obliged. He needed to see it, to know that Tyler's body was down there, even if his soul was not.

Even though I am twenty-three years old, since that day I have struggled with the physicality of Tyler's death as well. I thought seeing Tyler's body would finally make my subconscious understand that he was gone, but just like Hudson, it confused my perception of his death even more.

It started when I touched his hand. It was cold and hard and covered in makeup and did not feel like a hand. I will never forget the rigid, synthetic feeling of Tyler's hand, and will probably still have nightmares about that inhuman texture until the day I leave this Earth. Then, when I went to kiss the top of his head, there was a fleeting moment when my lips touched his hair and I felt like he might still be alive. The sensation of Tyler's signature curls (almost identical to my own), still completely as they were, was so unmistakably Tyler that I thought, *No, he's still here!* But then my lips hit the top of his head and it felt like I was kissing a boulder. The rapid succession of these two opposing sensations sent me reeling. How could those curls still exist, bouncy and wild as they always were, yet the rest of him was so changed? It made no sense to me. He was half there, half not.

Since the funeral, I have had the most irrational thoughts about the continued existence of Tyler's body. The detectives said things like "brain swelling," and "fluid in the lungs," and it confused me—those were not words I associated with Tyler. Then I accidentally stumbled across the details of autopsies and embalmment while reading a book and lost my shit. How could Tyler come back to us if he didn't have any blood? And while visiting the gravesite comforts my mom, I just stare at the dirt thinking we buried him alive. When summer turned to fall, I worried every night if Tyler was cold because we only buried him in a Hawaiian shirt and a suit jacket.

I have the same thoughts when I think about his belongings. I didn't want any of his clothes or items because I felt like we were stealing from him. My mom contemplated returning the back-to-school clothes the two had just bought together, and I couldn't believe how cruel she was being to Tyler. He was going to need those when he went back to school. He picked them out, they were his, and he would be upset if she gave them back, right? While my mom wears his sweatshirts and fleeces every day, I can't bring myself to. The lone sweater I took back to California with me still hangs in my closet, untouched, waiting for him.

When I told my mom some of this, she looked at my angrily and asked, "Would you rather we have cremated him?"

The answer to this question is no because setting him on fire wouldn't be any better than him decaying naturally. I hate the physicality of death, the fact that when you die, you leave a body behind that must be dealt with. I don't wish we cremated him, but I do wish his body just disappeared. I wish he went off to college or heaven forever, leaving no physical trace behind. He had so much energy when he was alive that it was legitimately unsettling to see him completely still like that. I wish I didn't have to see Tyler as an empty shell, stiff, jaw wired shut, full of formaldehyde. And I wish Hudson didn't have to see it either.

What I do want is for Hudson and myself to remember the good parts, the face full of life, our favorite brother. My biggest fear is for Hudson to grow up and forget Tyler, for him to be an adult one day and tell people, "I had a brother who died when I was little, but I don't really remember him." Tyler was fundamental to my and all our siblings' development as people, and I want, I *need*, Hudson to feel the same way.

I can only thank Lindsey for what I bemoaned the entire time I knew her: taking pictures of every single moment of our lives. No trip to McDonald's was too unimportant for Lindsey to snap a family photo, and while it drove the rest of us nuts at the time, it's now the most precious source of Tyler content we have. These seemingly mundane, everyday moments are even more special now—I am so glad we are not limited to formal pictures of birthdays and graduations. Looking at them together now, I can't help but think that they will help us remember all the little parts about Tyler, so much more than we might otherwise have. Hudson even once proclaimed to a family friend, "You know why my mom takes pictures all the time? So we can have memories like we do of my Aunt LaLa and brother Tyler!"

Most adults have a few memories dating back to when they are three or four years old. However, some of these memories are implanted, a result of stories or photos shared and imagined to the point that the person falsely procures the memory as authentically their own (Association for Psychological Science, 2018). I don't particularly care which of these is the case for Hudson. The pictures and videos are a representation of how things were, and if they can help Hudson understand who Tyler was better than his own memories, I welcome them fully. Tyler died when Hudson was five years old, so between his personal memories and Lindsey's hoard of visual aids, I have the utmost faith that he will still grow up knowing his big brother.

After writing the initial draft of this chapter, I sat down one day to watch *Star Wars: The Last Jedi* with Hudson. He was yammering on and on, telling me trivia facts about every scene and character in the movie. I, unlike Tyler, tuned out for most of it.

"You know a lot about *Star Wars*!" I finally exclaimed. I, myself, have only minimal knowledge of the franchise and had nothing more insightful to contribute.

"My brother Tyler taught me about it," he said offhandedly, like I should have already known this. "I watch *Star Wars* so I can remember him…sister, why are you crying?"

I hugged Hudson tighter than I ever had in my life. This five-year-old goofball is just as committed to keeping Tyler's memory alive as I am, and together, we will make sure Tyler is with us forever.

VII

—

The best part of writing this book has been learning about Tyler from many different perspectives. I now know about him as a son, best friend, even boyfriend, which has been equal parts interesting and gross. My own stories are limited to the viewpoint of an older sister, but Tyler had other siblings who played important roles in his life as well. While we each have our own unique relationship with him, there is a shared experience of what it's like to have Tyler Young as a brother.

There is one story that I think describes who Tyler was as a brother to me more than any other. This memory is permanently ingrained in my mind, and even in death, I still haven't forgiven him for it.

I was a senior in high school, he an eighth grader. At this point, Tyler was really into golf, and was in a junior league that held practices and competitions in the area. There were two practice courses: one at West Park, five minutes from our house, the other, Raspberry Falls, his more common venue, another twenty-minute drive north on Route 15. Being the ultimate space cadet, Tyler left a club at practice and needed someone to drive him to pick it up. Newly licensed, I was responsible for the ride.

"I was supposed to be on my way already!" I whined, much preferring to spend time with my then-boyfriend over running errands for Tyler.

"So leave right after," my mom wasn't budging.

Tyler got in the passenger seat, and I begrudgingly began driving us toward Raspberry Falls, which sat in the back of a pricey neighborhood. As we passed West Park, I sighed, whining about how far away Raspberry Falls was and how annoying the drive was. Tyler agreed, and we passed the next twenty minutes with me being passive aggressive, pointing out how late I was for my date, Tyler apologizing accordingly. When we entered the Raspberry Falls neighborhood, we pointed at many of the huge homes, talking about our dream house and what designs we did or didn't like. We finally made it to the golf course parking lot, turned into a spot, and put the car in park.

"Okay," I sighed. "Go get your club."

"Why are we at Raspberry Falls?" Tyler asked. "I left my golf club at West Park."

After a phone call that consisted of me screaming into the phone and my mom telling me through tears of laughter that she couldn't punish Tyler for being a dumbass, we made our way back to West Park, and I ended up being over an hour late for my plans.

Tyler was truly the epitome of an annoying brother. I have known this since the day he was born, and while there was a time when it was just Tyler and I, once our parents got remarried, there were six new siblings to join in on or put up with Tyler's brotherly antics. My mom married Jeff, who had Lauren (Tyler's age), Dalton (a year below), and Briley (three years below Dalton) from his previous marriage. My dad married Lindsey, who had Connor (my age) and Courtney

(Tyler's age) from previous relationships, and together had Hudson (fourteen years behind Courtney and Tyler). TL;DR: Tyler quickly went from having one sibling to seven. Since both our parents got into their new relationships while I was in sixth grade, Tyler in second, we lived most of our conscious lives with the blended family dynamic, and the other kids got to have their own collection of Tyler stories.

Tyler and I were close with all our siblings pretty much from the time our parents started dating to the present (with the brief exception of early middle school when my stepbrother Connor and I were consistently on the brink of committing homicide). Tyler was especially close with Dalton and Courtney, the two closest to him in age who didn't find his troublemaking horrifying like Lauren did. Courtney now had a sibling her age, and Dalton, who had spent most of his childhood choosing between playing princesses with his sisters or not playing at all, finally had a brother.

Dalton and Tyler became best buddies and confidants, making goofy YouTube videos or Vines (for my Zillennials out there) and exploring the woods without a fairy costume in sight. Tyler was more rambunctious than Dalton at the time and ended up roping him into some illicit behavior. If I thought one little brother was annoying, two were a nightmare. Their quick brotherly friendship meant that they fed off each other's miscreant energy, encouraging pure chaos in each other. After the first two years of our parents' dating, their silliness reached its peak in a particularly eventful day filled with theft and vandalism.

At age fourteen I was going through a gardening phase and had planted some cucumbers that had done extremely well. They were almost ripe enough to eat, and the day I went to pick them, I discovered that they had disappeared.

My mom consoled me and reminded me that we lived in the woods—there were hungry deer all around, and next time we would put some wire over top to prevent it from happening again. You'll imagine my surprise when elementary-aged Dalton and Tyler came prancing through the front door with about twenty dollars' worth of small bills between them.

"Where have you two been?" my mom asked, knowing that Tyler spontaneously generating money could never be a good sign.

"Making money!" he beamed. "The neighbors bought all the cucumbers we had!"

Tyler died very young, but he could have died even younger had my mom not held me back from attacking him that day. I have still never felt a violent rage quite like the one Tyler inspired that day. My mom made them give me the money they earned from selling the black-market cucumbers and demanded an apology from each. I was furious for the rest of the day, until the hilarity of what happened next overshadowed my anger. We thought the day's drama was over when we got a call from a neighbor who claimed he had seen Dalton and Tyler vandalizing cars promptly after their door-to-door farmer's market scandal.

"WHAT?" my mom gasped, her mind filled with images of slashed tires and huge insurance bills. "*What did they do to the cars?*"

"Well…" the neighbor sounded half concerned, half trying not to laugh. "There's…pink frosting all over them, and mushrooms stuck to the frosting. And maybe some Sharpie penis drawings?"

Fourth- and fifth-grade Dalton and Tyler admitted their crimes and made similar reparations to the neighbors as they did to me. This became a constant pattern—Tyler coming up with some harebrained scheme, Dalton tagging along for the adventure. Much to the rest of the family's dismay, this pattern continued through the rest of their relationship, completely untouched by the effects of maturity. In high school, the two often did things like breaking into a half-constructed house to get shelter from a snowstorm, setting off a homemade bomb in the backyard, or flying a drone and losing it in the woods.

While their annoying little brother behavior never changed, their social lives did. Tyler remained a goofy, energetic smart kid who always had friends, yet was never part of a particular crowd. He was entertaining and had pretty normal interactions with kids his age, but he would never be considered popular. Dalton, on the other hand, is straight out of an '80s high school movie. He is six feet, three inches tall and good looking, had a string of girlfriends, was the starting pitcher for his high school's baseball team, and maintained a squad of other popular boys in his grade. If they really were in an '80s movie, Dalton would have bullied the crap out of a kid like Tyler, who almost exclusively wore Hawaiian shirts and did calculus for fun.

Not only did Dalton refrain from bullying Tyler, but he also kept him close and even integrated him within his own friend group whenever possible. They did not attend the same high school, but during weekend hangouts and birthday parties, Dalton always included Tyler in whatever he and his friends were doing. It was never out of pity—he genuinely loved spending time with him, and his friends grew to enjoy the presence of Dalton's quirky brother as well. They came to Tyler's funeral and were sad for themselves as well as Dalton. My mom always credits Dalton for this kindness, appreciating his inclusivity and thanking him for bringing Tyler out of his shell, but Dalton views the situation as exactly the opposite.

"I don't know why your mom always says that. I was *not* always like this," he told me a few months after Tyler died and my mom had just alluded to this facet of their relationship. "I was so quiet as a kid, super awkward, and Tyler was way more outgoing than I was. I had a crush on this girl in middle school but had no idea how to talk to her, so Tyler coached me on what to text her and made me so much more confident. It was *him* who made *me* more social."

Dalton truly looked up to his older brother, and even after so much time and change from the days of grand theft cucumber, he still loved him and credited a large part of his development to Tyler.

When I first heard the news of Tyler's death, I really wanted to talk to Dalton about it. All day, I just wanted to comfort him and have him comfort me, but I had to wait. I was the second person to get the phone call, but my mom and Jeff wanted to ensure the other kids received the news the right way, in person. It wasn't until I was on my five-hour flight back home that Jeff went over to Dalton, Lauren, and Briley's mom's house to break the news.

"He asked us to come out on the back porch," Dalton remembers. "I knew something bad happened. The last time my mom and dad made us sit on the back porch, they were telling us they were getting divorced."

The second porch conversation was the only time Dalton had ever seen his dad truly cry, and one of the few occasions he had seen Briley or Lauren cry. It set him off on his own emotional downward spiral. He left the house to be alone for a while and to reminisce on the incredible brother he finally gained, and now lost. He had it good for so long, but now that Tyler is gone, he's stuck with *three* sisters with no brotherly barrier in between.

On the other side of the family, Courtney was taking things equally as hard. She had to get the news through a phone call, as she was already back at college in Kentucky. When she found out, she panicked, not even knowing what to think or how to feel. Our nearby aunt and uncle were there for her and helped her calm down and get on a flight to Virginia for the funeral. Of all my siblings, Courtney is the one who seems to cry as much as I do—she always checks in on me and outwardly expresses her sadness and how much she misses him pretty regularly. She reminds me that it is okay to grieve and not be okay.

Tyler had entered her life when she was too young to understand what divorce was or the nuances of a new family, and she just went with the flow because it's what the adults decided. She and Tyler caused less monetary damage than he and Dalton, but they still became quick companions. Nights at my dad's townhouse were mostly spent making a fort out of the papasan chair to hide in while they stayed up all night watching George Lopez reruns, in a simple bliss that only children can attain.

When I was in eighth grade, Tyler in fourth, Lindsey and my dad moved into a house together in our school district, meaning Courtney and Connor had to transfer to Tyler's and my school. While they were always playmates at home, as they got older, Courtney and Tyler started naturally hanging out with the same friends. One time, the two separately asked our parents if they could go to a friend's house, left in separate cars, and ended up at the same place. This was when their friendship became real, not just a childhood companionship of convenience. We sometimes joked that they were the twins because they became so in sync, sharing secrets and making the same annoying noises at the dinner table. My dad and Lindsey spent their entire careers working with middle schoolers, but nothing could agitate them quite like Tyler and Courtney making seal noises while we were trying to eat.

The twins got to graduate high school together and see each other off to college, Tyler in Chicago, Courtney in Lexington. In fact, the last time they saw each other in person, the family was helping Courtney move into her sophomore year apartment at the University of Kentucky. The seat assignments worked out so that Tyler and Courtney rode in the same car alone for eight hours together, something they had never done before.

"We never got to do stuff like that," she told me recently with a smile. "We just bonded. He kept asking me to buy him chew. It was so gross, but he let me listen to my own music the whole way, which was rare because he usually demands that we listen to the worst rap music he can find."

This memory was a testament to the loving relationships Tyler maintained with his siblings regardless of how much they grew or where they lived. Both Dalton and Courtney had Tyler as a brother from the innocent childhood days up until the day he died. They were both up close and personal with his journey along the way, but perhaps because of the nature of the sibling dynamic, never quite knew how they could help Tyler's struggles. Tyler shared more about his substance abuse issues with the two of them than he ever did with me, probably because of their closeness in age—I was more likely to get him in trouble than sneak around with him.

"It started when we were so young," Dalton told me. "I remember one time he showed me something that he said was meth, but I had no idea if it was real or not, so I didn't say anything to the parents. I also just didn't understand any of that stuff."

"We drank cough syrup together once," Courtney recalled. "We were so little; I didn't really know what I was doing. We drank it and I felt so weird, and we ended up getting caught and getting in huge trouble. It seemed like this funny thing to do at the time, so when he did even more later, I didn't really know that it was actually dangerous. I was also twelve, so when I saw him doing bad things, I didn't want to tattle on him."

Tyler's loss of innocence was hard to understand for the two people who had once shared that innocence with him. Neither Dalton nor Courtney knew half as much about drugs as Tyler did, and didn't want to jeopardize the closeness they shared by ratting him out, especially since they didn't think he was in a life-threatening situation. Tyler maintained his connection with his family while struggling with drugs on the side, mentioning it sometimes but never doing something frightening in front of them or showing them how dangerous it really was. He was a master at sneaking around and explaining his actions in a way that reassured you he had everything under control. Even when Tyler's problems escalated to the point that he had to enter rehab, none of the siblings could really rationalize what was happening.

Courtney remembers shock at seeing Tyler in the psychiatric ward before he entered his first recovery program. This was the first time she had ever seen Tyler blatantly out of control, in a setting designed to help people with serious problems.

"The place was awful," she said. "We visited him, and I just cried the whole time. It didn't seem like he should be there."

"We all went to visit him in rehab that one Christmas," Dalton reminded me. "And yeah, we were visiting him in rehab, but he was still Tyler. He seemed the same, so it was hard to think that he was really in big trouble."

As strange as it sounds, my siblings' grief helps me in my own. Not that I am glad to see them so sad, but seeing this pain reminds me of how great a brother Tyler is. For a while it was just me and Tyler, but he got to be a brother to quite a few other siblings by the time he died. In fact, each of my siblings has eased some of my grief through our common experiences. My older stepbrother, Connor, shares the same guilty feeling I keep having. That as the older siblings we had a duty to guide and protect Tyler. The fact that I don't blame Connor and he doesn't blame me is more comforting than anything an outsider could say on the subject.

Briley and Lauren have the funniest stories about Tyler, reinforcing my ideas of how silly and fun he was. Tyler used to walk in a room and simply say, "Lamp," and Briley, the stoic one in the family, would collapse in a fit of laughter. We still have no idea how the inside joke started, but he could make her laugh while the rest of us failed miserably. Every year on Lauren's birthday, our family still watches a candid video Dalton once recorded: Tyler steals the TV remote and changes the channel while Lauren was watching a show. You can't see her, but you can hear an almost inhuman voice growl, *Give me the fucking clicker!* Tyler immediately returns the remote, downright scared. No one can make you laugh or piss you off like a brother, and I am so fortunate to see other sisters go through the "Tyler Experience."

More than anything, we are lucky that we never lost Tyler while he was still alive. Some who struggle with addiction resent their families, run away, or otherwise have moments of huge conflict with those they love as a result of their mental dependency on a substance that requires priority before anything else. Many who suffer from drug dependencies withdraw from their family members and friends, lying or becoming outwardly aggressive toward those who show any sign of noticing the addiction or wanting to help (Sakar, 2013). Documented in *Beautiful Boy* and *Tweak*, Nic Sheff himself ran away from his family, choosing to live on the streets of New York City rather than accepting their offers to send him to a recovery institution—and this is not uncommon (Sheff, 2008 and Sheff, 2008).

Tyler never turned on us—while he hid some of his problems, he did so more out of love and not wanting to hurt us than from malice or mistrust. He willingly accepted punishment when he was caught and assistance when the situation became dire. Until the moment his soul left his body, he remained the Tyler we all knew and loved. I don't know what stopped him from experiencing this family conflict or estrangement common in those who struggle with addiction, but I thank God every day that he never turned away from us.

We are extremely lucky in this way because there really aren't many bad memories of Tyler to wrestle with while we grieve. Among seven siblings, he didn't have a complicated relationship with a single one of them. No estrangements or traumatic, drug-fueled conflicts muddle our perception of him. As I watch the others cry over him, I am so thankful that they are able to cry purely for the soul of my baby brother, without the painful, unintended clashes that so many others in our position have to contend with. We were downright lucky that his symptoms and struggles never manifested themselves that way, that nearly every encounter we ever had with Tyler was one of love and brotherhood.

VIII

———

While Tyler's struggles were terrifyingly present for the members of our immediate family, they were more of a source of frustration and confusion for those outside the nuclear homes in Virginia. My mom and dad were constantly updating the rest of us on his progress or missteps during and after rehab, causing a never-ending cycle of anxiety for me, my stepparents, and other siblings. Due to divorce, remarriage, and the fact that my great grandparents on my dad's side had seventeen children, we have quite a few extended family members who care about Tyler, but from a distance.

Our family comes mostly from central Illinois and eastern Texas, with branches extending all over the country. While we are close with my dad's siblings, parents, and several of his seventy-eight first cousins, the three extended family members most present to Tyler and me were all from my mom's side—her mom (our Grandma Joyce), her brother (our Uncle Phil), and her uncle (Uncle Tim, technically our great-uncle). They all cared about Tyler in their own remote ways.

My Grandma Joyce is the most timid, never-ask-anyone-for-anything person I've ever met. She rarely calls first, never wanting to waste your time or be a burden, no matter how many times you tell her you love talking to her. It is not surprising that she never pressed my mom or me for Tyler updates, even though she would become deeply frustrated by the fact that she was never quite in the loop.

"I always knew there were problems," she told me while she was in town for his funeral. "I just never knew the extent. I never knew *this* was a possibility."

She later told me about how much she worried about both Tyler's safety as well as my mom's emotional state. She was caught in a delicate balance of wanting to know answers about her grandson while not wanting to make things worse for my already struggling mother. She offered support when the opportunity arose but did not go out of her way to uncover the scary realities of what we were facing. She would answer my mom's weekly phone calls and share a sympathetic word when prompted. She never probed, though, or asked for information that was not offered organically.

Phil was often just as goofy as Tyler and always seemed to have a soft spot for his peer in annoying brotherhood. He drove from New York and Massachusetts all the way to Tyler's New England rehab facility on two separate business trips just to visit and show that he cared. On Tyler's last Christmas, when the family spent a few nights in a Chicago Airbnb, he asked Tyler to take him on a tour of the University of Illinois Chicago, where Tyler had just finished his first semester. While Tyler's struggles were a semi-mystery to Phil, who just like my grandma was one layer removed from the situation, and my brother was sometimes difficult to relate to, Phil did make an active effort to show Tyler that he was there for him beyond the extent of familial obligation.

Tim was in a similar boat as Phil. He is known as the life of the family party, always up for a game of pool or a glass of something much stronger than anything I can stomach. In this way, he sometimes felt connected to the rebellious Tyler, but Tim had never ventured into behavior as dangerous or scary as Tyler's. His antics were largely harmless and revolved around socialization and fun ways to pass his free time, not as a risky or solitary way to escape the torments of his own mind. Tim wrote Tyler letters and tried to talk to him when he could get ahold of him, but he ultimately was still living halfway across the country in Colorado, getting information secondhand whenever he chatted with my mom, dad, or me.

Information was spread through secondary means in part because of Tyler's own aloofness and lack of motivation to reach out and communicate with others. Since he was a young child, all three of our close relatives recall finding it difficult to connect with him on a meaningful level. While he was always charismatic or goofy, he was not particularly warm or open about how he was feeling or what troubles were ailing him. He was happy and fun without displaying emotional depth. What was most present in child Tyler was an internal curiosity and an external chaos.

Tim and Phil both reminded me of two of Tyler's most curious and chaotic childhood behaviors: his obsessive personality and his sneakiness. He was never passively interested in anything but would become wholeheartedly consumed by whatever hobby caught his attention. Whether it was Eminem's music, Tarantino movies, or the entire *Star Wars* universe, Tyler was all in, able to recite obscure facts that even the most loyal fan wouldn't know at a moment's notice.

One particularly obsessive phase revolved around money. Our family used to play a dice game during Christmases or other gatherings; everyone starts with three dollar bills, and depending on how you roll, you could keep your money, give it to other players, or put it in the pot in the middle—the last person standing wins the entire pot. There is an infamous photo of seven-year-old Tyler one of these Christmases, scooping up thirty dollars' worth of dollar bills after winning the game, smiling like he had just won the lottery while the adults looked on in amusement.

On another Christmas trip, Tim caught Tyler in his office, digging through drawers and shelves.

"What are you looking for?" he asked, concerned.

"Nothing," Tyler responded, and this was entirely true. He had no hidden agenda, nor did he expect to find anything in particular—he was simply curious (nosy). This action had nothing to do with his previous money obsession, but was a separate, intense desire to learn and know and stay busy.

Some of his behavior ventured into destructive or potentially dangerous territory. Tim holds Tyler accountable for several hundred dollars' worth of property damage. For years, Christmas was always held at Tim's house in Illinois, and each year one of Tyler's explorations would end in a few broken household items.

Even though Tim suffered some financial loss at the hands of Tyler, Phil was the one who experienced the pinnacle of prepubescent Tyler mischief. The two were in the parking lot of an airport car rental facility, and Phil got out of the car to initiate the return process. Tyler, at this point less than ten years old, somehow managed to put the car in drive. When Phil turned around, the car was slowly rolling away, Tyler's grinning face peeking out of the driver seat. Phil managed to fling the door open and stop the car, but the misadventures remained a characteristic part of the Tyler experience. It was hard to know what he was going to get into next, but after years of phone calls from the school, frustrated babysitters, and one horribly flooded basement, he earned a bit of a reputation.

As hectic and gossip worthy as these events were, they did not shed light into Tyler's internal psyche or personal motivations. To the casual observer Tyler was an extremely active child and young adult, but he was never active in communicating with others. If you never called Tyler, he would never call you. If you never questioned him, he would never explain his emotions or thought processes. He was a tornado, a mysterious one, and he didn't grow out of it. At age nineteen, Grandma Joyce was still tiptoeing around, trying to gain information without intruding; Tim was attempting to probe Tyler through letters and late-night conversations; and Phil was offering his company and support, even when he didn't really know what was going on.

Tyler and I are night and day in this sense. My grandma and I are extremely close. We chat on the phone at least once a week, and she is up to speed on everything from my career choices to my love life. Tim, a former professor of political science and my joint academic idol/therapist, was my guiding light as I went through the agony that is deciding to go back to grad school. Phil and I simply have a lot in common—he covers the Twins for the *Minneapolis Star Tribune* and actually got me tickets to Game 7 of the 2016 World Series when the Cubs won for the first time in 108 years. Tyler loved these family members, but without the obvious common grounds that I was lucky enough to share with them.

Tyler also never exhibited any of his most self-harming behaviors around these loved ones. While our immediate family sometimes caught him at his most vulnerable because of our sheer proximity to him, it was easier to hide his addiction from people he only saw in person a few times a year. To my knowledge, the only time any of them were ever around him while he was under the influence was the Christmas before he died, when I found him in our shared room, fucked up on God knows what at four in the morning. Even then, it was I who discovered him, and my mom who helped me clean up his vomit and get him to bed. Our other family members did not see this event in person, just heard about it from us the next day after seeing him tiptoeing around the house, hungover. The ugly reality remained a rumor for them.

This is not to say that Tyler was a recluse, or that he did not enjoy interacting with his broader family. When he was required to tag along to family events, he was present, charismatic, and game for anything. During Tyler's last Christmas, Tim's grandchildren followed him around the entire time we were together, hanging onto his every word and making him play with them. He is also closer to my dad's side of the family than I am because he happened to be around for more family time while I was at college or in California. Shortly before Tyler died, he, my dad, Lindsey, and Hudson went to Illinois to visit my dad's dad, and the photo evidence shows Tyler drinking root beer floats with Hudson and riding horses (even though he's allergic). Tyler was *fun*. His constant jokes, stories, and go-getter attitude made him a very entertaining person to be around.

The stark contrast between Tyler's fun, family-friendly persona and the scattered knowledge of Tyler's troubles generated mixed opinions from family members. Grandma Joyce really had no opinion as she never knew enough to be qualified to consider his chances of survival. Phil was ever the optimist—he always believed in Tyler's smarts and free will to pull him out of harm's way. He was still young; he would grow out of it. Tim was perhaps the only one who genuinely worried that Tyler might not make it. When I asked him about it, he asked me a question that I, myself, had wondered many times.

"Even if he did grow up," Tim began. "I always wondered what he would do."

While I never consciously thought Tyler would die, I admit that I never imagined the future. I could not picture us sitting together in our forties, watching our kids play with each other. I couldn't imagine him holding down a stable career or family, completely over his addiction problems and fully in control of his own hyperactive mind. I had a mixture of Phil's naivete in the present with Tim's skepticism of the future, yet never staunchly in one camp or the other. If I'm being honest, I was very focused on the now: Would Tyler pass this semester, would he be sober during COVID-19, was he still attending AA meetings? My thoughts never went too far forward. I was taking it one crisis at a time.

I ended up telling both Grandma Joyce and Phil that Tyler had died. I stopped before I got to Tim, realizing that I had no details and should probably stop blabbing without direction from my mom. Grandma Joyce barely said a word when I told her, completely shocked and confused. Phil, however, was a nightmarishly painful call to make.

We had talked on the phone just the day before, where I told him about how my pet snake had died. I had just bought him, a rare and expensive ball python from a fancy Los Angeles reptile breeder, and he had a freak brain problem that gave him a deadly aneurism two days after I purchased him. Phil, a proud turtle father for over twenty years, poked fun at me for my apparent bad luck with pets. The breeder had replaced my snake, and he joked that maybe this one would last a week. When I called him to tell him about Tyler, he was still in the jovial mood I had left him in the day before.

"Phil," I gasped through sobs. "I just got off the phone... he's dead."

"Already?!" he laughed. My stomach dropped—he still thought I was talking about the snake.

"Who...who do you think I'm talking about?" I whispered.

"Your snake..." he trailed off, and I could tell that he was no longer confident in his assumption.

"Noooo," I moaned. "I'm talking about Tyler."

"No," I could hear it in his voice, that same blood-curdling realization that had me screaming on the floor twenty minutes before.

He quickly passed the phone to my Aunt Linda, who had lost her sister years before and knew how to handle me in my immediate panic. We talked on the phone for an hour before I had to leave for my flight, me speed-walking around my neighborhood while she calmed me down.

Grandma Joyce, Phil, and Tim, all made it to the funeral and have since been an enormous source of comfort to my mom and me. I remember the night Phil and my grandma showed up together. They had driven all day from Minnesota and Illinois to avoid flying during COVID-19 and embraced my mom as soon as they walked in and set down their bags. I will never forget the pang of jealousy I felt watching my mom hug her brother.

I will never hug my brother again.

Since then, they have been one of the biggest sources of comfort to me. They are the keepers of so many childhood stories, some that I was too young to remember. Through them, I relive the days where I played and wreaked havoc with my baby brother, not a worry in the world. I love hearing stories about the two of us making forts or sliding down the stairs on couch cushions; because it reminds me that even though much of Tyler's adolescent and adult life was hard, there were truly some pure and blissful moments. There was a time when the Young children were just children, crazy little kids with a whole life ahead of them. Who could watch us playing Guitar Hero and making each other drink toilet water and think that one day I would have to grow up all alone?

This might sound twisted, but it comforts me to see my broader family mourning Tyler. It brought me comfort when Phil cried, or when Tim told me he was taking Tyler's death extremely hard—it meant that he still mattered to those who didn't live with him. Grandma Joyce and I had a moment I'll never forget when shopping for a funeral dress together. She offered to go with me at a time in the pre-funeral week when there was so much activity going on. It was a good opportunity to be helpful without getting in the way. I found a different dress, just something cute and unrelated, and she decided to buy it for me, completely unprompted. I thanked her, and her reply brought me to tears.

"Well, I guess I only have one grandchild to spoil now," she told me. I could see in her face how sad this fact made her and how happy she was to spend some time with her remaining grandchild. She and I have a long tradition of going shopping together whenever she is in town, so this gesture felt like the best way she could think of to comfort me on terms we were both familiar with.

My family also reminds me that none of us know everything about Tyler. Some of their frustration comes from not being at the source of the action, but some of it also comes from that aloof, always-on-the-go nature that Tyler carried everywhere he went. Especially since his death, friends have shared stories about him that I had never heard, and I realize that Tyler was such a big, complex person, not just my little brother, nor did he belong to any one person. Grandma Joyce would never know everything about him, but then neither would I, and that's okay.

I want to make Tyler proud and do the things he will never get to do. Grandma Joyce only has my mom and Phil, Phil does not have biological children of his own, and I am now my mom's only living child. Tim has a daughter and two grandkids but has never treated Tyler and me like anything less than his own grandkids. I don't want to put pressure on myself, but I want to generate enough pride and happiness to ease the immense loss of potential that Tyler left in our family, even if it's just a little. I want to have a beautiful family and name a child after Tyler—I think that would make my Grandma smile (I'm serious, the fact that I don't have a boyfriend at the ripe old age of twenty-three sets off alarm bells in her head). I want to get a PhD like my genius brother undoubtedly would have done and share my love of learning with students like Tim did his whole adult life (but focus on subjects more interesting than political science). Finally, I want to write a book about Tyler's life and be a published writer like Phil (I'd say I got this one in the bag).

IX

I cannot emphasize enough how smart Tyler was. Despite my own academic success, I am objectively the dumb kid in the family. Tyler was a certified, Mensa-level genius, which we discovered when he took several personality tests through his doctor around the time he went to rehab. While trying to uncover some reasons for his anxiety and substance abuse issues, his doctors were blown away by how freakishly intelligent he was. In high school, my mom would go up to his room to say goodnight to him while he was "finishing up" a few math problems, then return in the morning to wake him up, only to find him in the same position, having stayed up all night doing math for fun. He published a math theorem before his eighteenth birthday, and his Christmas wish lists were always full of items like ten-by-ten Rubik's cubes, chemistry sets, and graduate-level textbooks.

When he was sixteen and I was twenty, our grandpa and Phil took us to see the Toronto Blue Jays play the Cubs while we visited them in Chicago. While we watched the game, Tyler sat on the ground, used his seat as a desk, took out his phone, and started scribbling equations on the back of his scorecard. We had no clue what he was doing until he casually looked up sometime in the third inning and declared,

"Based on temperature, elevation, and wind velocity, it would be the easiest to hit a homerun in the Oakland Coliseum right now." We thanked him for this useless information and continued to watch the game while he squirmed with boredom for the remaining six innings.

His genius, while impressive, was often paired with a complete restlessness in everyday situations. He could not relax and enjoy a day at Wrigley Field like the rest of us. His mind felt like a gift and a curse, being one of his best qualities as well as his biggest challenge. He could sometimes only satiate the mental torrent by doing these extreme or unnecessary feats of intelligence—the only way to make his brain tired enough to go to sleep was to stay up all night doing math, and the only way for him to get through a tearfully boring baseball game was to come up with a complex and irrelevant equation to solve.

At sixteen years old he was already done with BC Calculus, taking classes like Linear Algebra and Multivariable Calculus at the local community college. I spoke with his last high school math teacher, Mrs. Hefty, who remembers being constantly amazed at his pure mathematical enthusiasm. I had to get a tutor to pass precalculus and switched to statistics as soon as I could, so I had never met her before this meeting. When reflecting on Tyler as a student, she said he was one of only two or three students she had met in her entire career whom she genuinely believed was smarter than she was. She boasts her own impressive math career; nonetheless, she was continuously in awe of Tyler's emphasis on not only understanding the material, but also his thinking through alternative methods and questioning the theoretical ideas way beyond the scope of the curriculum. While sometimes annoying, his raw intelligence and curiosity to learn beyond the course requirements were extremely admirable. She described Tyler's death and consequent loss of brainpower as simply "a waste," a familiar sentiment to the family of the dead who want Tyler to be cherished and remembered outside of our own household.

At Tyler's high school graduation, one of his friends told me in private that another classmate of theirs had expressed shock at seeing Tyler walk across the stage. He had not been in the building since the spring of his junior year, and while many people knew he was in a recovery facility, they did not realize he was keeping up with school and making a better life for himself.

"I thought he dropped out," she had apparently said. "Wasn't he a druggie or something?"

This sentiment completely guts me, but it is not uncommon. Stigmas around those with drug addiction have always existed, even in the health care field. Those with addiction often report unhelpful encounters with health care professionals, from having their health issues not taken seriously to outright dismissal. For instance, during hospital overcrowding in the COVID-19 pandemic, many hospitals would use a person's addiction problem as a reason to refuse service (Volkow, 2020).

There is a common misconception that the addicted person is a bad person, a "bum," or somehow has a choice in the matter, that drugs do not literally rewire your brain into creating a biological need for the substance (Kosten and George, 2002). The reasons people try drugs in the first place are horribly misconstrued as well—some become addicted from a legally prescribed painkiller, or, in Tyler's case, from using it as a means of self-medicating his own serious mental health struggles. Drug abuse, especially opioid abuse, is also becoming heavily suburban, not just a problem for inner-city, lower income, or delinquent populations (Cicero, Ellis, Surratt, et al, 2014).

To hear someone assume that Tyler's entire being was centered around his drug abuse, that he was defined by his drug use and nothing else, crushed my heart. My brilliant brother, who was being incredibly strong and fighting an enormous battle, was viewed as a flunky by his peers. It seemed as if once drugs entered the picture, they overshadowed every other aspect of Tyler's life and personality.

Little did people know that not a single thing he did, even his drug-related endeavors, was removed from his genius. He used his mathematical, technical, and chemical skills to make meth in our basement, learned how to scramble his GPS location to sneak around without getting caught, and sometimes used household products to get high, knowing the exact chemical properties of each. He lost his virginity on a cafeteria table at a Princeton summer camp, for God's sake. No matter how innocent or dangerous his actions, everything was tangled with his constantly moving mind.

This infamous Princeton camp was part of a sequence of brainiac summer enrichment programs he completed throughout middle and high school: one at Princeton, one at Yale, and one at UCLA. His last year at UCLA, before his sophomore year of high school, our entire family visited Los Angeles to pick him up from camp and spend a week sightseeing. He showed us around campus with an intense sense of pride. It was this trip that inspired me to move to LA myself after undergrad and apply to UCLA's PhD program (I got rejected). To this day, I am still living in the intellectual shadows of my fifteen-year-old brother.

This feeling that Tyler was way smarter than I was and most of the people helping him in his recovery journey was the main reason I felt he was always somewhat safe no matter what drugs he took. He knew the molecular components of every substance he ingested and sometimes even explained to me the best and/or safest ways to get high off certain things based on our own genetic makeup. He certainly knew way more about drugs than I or the rest of our family did, and while we were constantly worried about him, there was a sense that at least he knew what he was doing and would know if he was going too far. I categorized him as safer than the "everyday addict" because of this, thinking that others with less knowledge were more likely to miscalculate amounts and overdose or not recognize a drug that was laced. I believe Tyler also held onto this false sense of security. This flawed, protective genius, paired with the human sense of "it can't happen to me," ultimately became a recipe for disaster.

Tyler's genius brain also taught him how to lie and manipulate like a professional. While he never declared his hatred for his family, turned his back on us, or ran away from home, he did lie to our faces time after time. I like to believe he did it to spare our feelings or keep us from worrying, but the truth is probably less pleasant than that. My mom was the one he lied to the most, as she had most of the authority and paranoia. He knew how to touch her sympathy if he wanted money or attention and knew how to calm her fears if he was doing drugs or failing a class. Right when he entered rehab, he was encouraged to make a list of all the reasons why he wanted to get better, and the very first reason he listed was "my mother." He lied to her despite loving her, or sometimes *because* he loved her.

We caught him doing drugs many times, but there were so many more times we didn't. The night he relapsed over Christmas after his first semester in college, we truly thought it was his first relapse since leaving rehab, believing him when he said he was around substances all the time at school and had yet to partake. He could act sober or time his usage so we never noticed a change in behavior and knew to check in with a text or a phone call so we would think he was okay even when he was not. He also projected our anxiety back onto us sometimes, complaining that we never gave him space or trusted him when he was in fact relapsing that very moment.

It truly seemed like there were two completely separate Tylers, the Tyler we knew and loved, and the user Tyler he shielded us from. The number of times we now know he did drugs versus the times we caught him indicate that he kept most of his problems hidden and used his charisma and passive demeanor to lead us off the scent. The summer before he died, my mom kept telling him, "Tyler, we are always here for you, and if you have problems again, I will always be here to help you." Especially since it was his own cry for help that prompted us to enter him into a recovery program, there was a universal sense that he knew his limits and knew exactly what he was dealing with. Unsure of what was true and what was a lie, facing a now-legal adult with addiction issues, at some point we had to trust that Tyler would make the right decision, or at least ask for help if he couldn't.

We all felt a certain level of stupidity around Tyler. While we knew he shouldn't be doing drugs, it was hard to come up with a hard-hitting argument when the person you were trying to convince knew infinitely more about the subject than you did. I certainly didn't know the chemical compositions of these drugs, their potency, or their danger level. My parents' and my argument could be summed up with, "Drugs are bad," while Tyler could give a Socratic seminar about them.

One day while in rehab, Tyler got in trouble because one of the counselors discovered that he was "cheeking" his morning medication—pretending to swallow the pills, then stashing them in a hiding place so he could take a week's worth of pills at once. When my mom confronted him, he gave an answer that broke her heart.

"Why would you do that?" she asked, in a combination of shock and sadness.

"Because it's not enough," Tyler explained. "The dosage is so low, one pill doesn't do anything, but they won't up my prescription to the point that I actually feel it. So, I can either take it every day and feel nothing, or save it and take them all at once, so that one day a week I can feel normal like you."

Of all people, I thought of myself as the person who understood Tyler's reasoning behind using substances. While I have never needed to use drugs or alcohol to quell the buzzing of my own thoughts, my own obsessive-compulsive disorder diagnosis (classified as an anxiety disorder) is a testament to my own overwhelming thoughts. My anxiety issues mostly manifest themselves in excessive worrying about even the most minor events, intrusive thoughts, and the occasional panic attack. I think of myself as a more functional, dulled version of Tyler—while my anxiety problems are not as bad, I am not as wicked smart as he is, either.

In the effort to make non-addicts understand what might drive a person to begin abusing drugs, the best depiction of this buildup that I can offer comes from the 2019 HBO show *Euphoria*. In "Special Episode Part I: Rue," the protagonist, Rue, eats at a diner with Ali, a man who attends the same Alcoholics Anonymous group as she does and tries to help her overcome her reliance on drugs. He asks her why she recently relapsed, and their ensuing conversation made my jaw drop.

Ali: "Why'd you relapse?"

Rue: "I don't know, my mind was racing."

Ali: "About what?"

Rue: "Everything...I'm a piece of shit."

Ali: "You're not a drug addict because you're a piece of shit, you're a piece of shit because you're a drug addict.... You didn't come out of the womb an evil person. You, Rue, came out of the womb a beautiful baby girl, who unbeknownst to her had a couple of wires crossed. So when you tried drugs for the first time, it set something off in your brain that's beyond your control. And it isn't a question of willpower, it's not about how strong you are, you've been fighting a losing game since the first day you got high.... That is the disease of addiction. It is a degenerative disease. It is incurable. It is deadly, and it's no different from cancer. And you got it."

Tyler's brain, which was capable of complex math functions and hilarious wit, was also destroying itself. It made him miserable to even exist, so it's no wonder he tried drugs to make living a little bit more bearable. And as soon as he did for the first time, his brain's chemistry was rewired to crave more. That's why he liked math so much because it gave him an outlet for that intense energy. When he was laser-focused on some problem beyond my own comprehension, his brain was not spinning wildly out of control but flourishing.

This was a key issue to Tyler's recovery. While you could preach to him about the dangers of drugs all day, you couldn't rewire his brain to stop going at high speed at all times. And once you're addicted, your brain physically demands more. Even when he was sober, Tyler was on several anti-anxiety medications that didn't do much. The only things strong enough to give him some relief were illegal or abusable and therefore not something a doctor could prescribe him.

Ali was right—we were fighting a losing game. Short of lobotomizing Tyler, I'm not sure there was a way to cure him of his own demons. Sure, he learned plenty of coping techniques and tried to use math, chemistry, and music as an outlet, but overwhelmingly, he was still always hurting.

The alternative scenarios do not sit well with me. My tortured, genius brother would not have been the same person if he was neurotypical. It's part of who he was, and while I wished he lived a much longer life and found a way to live happily with his demons, I don't wish that he was a different person. His intelligence was a source of pride for him and gave him purpose. What he went through gave him strength and an empathy for others that only comes from battling your own hardships. The Tyler I know and love is an intellectual goofball, a kid with a golden heart who was in over his head. If you take away Tyler's big brain, you take away Tyler, and I wouldn't trade my brother for anything.

X

While his death in August 2020 was sudden and shocking, there was a time when our family worried intensely about Tyler's safety every day. His junior year in high school, about three years before his death, he started to get in trouble more often than he ever had previously. While I was away at college and didn't see much of the drama firsthand, every time I called my mom, she seemed to be constantly taking his phone away, grounding him, and generally worrying about him in a more serious way than I had ever noticed. I remember one phone call vividly.

Tyler's best friend Dean had just texted me the most horrifying picture I had ever seen in my life. It was circulating around the school and showed Tyler's arm next to a used needle. Even given Tyler's flair for the dramatic, I was shocked, and immediately showed our mom. She called him and said she was on her way to pick him up. He adamantly denied that he was doing drugs, saying the needle belonged to a friend with diabetes and the whole thing was set up as a joke. My mom describes the way he sounded on the phone as "dead sober," so she ultimately did not pull him out of school. Instead, she kept checking on him throughout the day until she was satisfied that he was not currently on some sort of hard drug.

Not a month later, I received another stressful call from my mom.

"Are you ready?" Mom asked in lieu of a proper greeting, prepping me for the news she was about to relay. "Tyler got suspended."

He and a friend got caught with marijuana in the school bathroom. Even though Tyler vehemently claimed it was not his, it was clear that his recklessness was starting to spiral out of control and have real consequences. His continued denial of his involvement did not save him, and the administration decided to suspend him. We didn't know it at the time, but the day he left to start his suspension would be his last day at Loudoun County High School ever.

My mom, not knowing what else to do with him, brought him into work with her, making him sit at an empty desk next to her and do homework until it was time for their weekly therapy session that evening. These sessions consisted of a one-on-one session between Tyler and his counselor before he joined a group of other struggling kids while my mom and Jeff joined the parents in their own group. After this session, a counselor stopped my mom on her way toward the door. She told my mom that in their one-on-one session, Tyler showed signs of being passively suicidal.

"He's not actively trying to kill himself," she explained. "But he has no fear of the risks involved in the things he's doing. He's dangerous to himself."

She recommended that Tyler go immediately to the hospital to be diagnosed, the first step toward longer, inpatient treatment. Tyler, who knew that telling a counselor potentially life-threatening information would allow them to break patient confidentiality and tell our mom, agreed that he needed help. He accepted the idea of him going to a psychiatric ward until they could figure out a more long-term solution.

Tyler admitted years later that he in fact did use his chemical knowledge to create a type of amphetamine in our basement, and on the day I received the picture from Dean, shot up speed (a form of methamphetamine) in the school bathroom. While amphetamines are a class of stimulants — some, like Adderall, even legal — methamphetamines have a structural difference that sends the substance to your brain more quickly and achieves a more intense high (Ashley Addiction Treatment, 2020). Tyler had finally scared even himself and raised his own hand for assistance with the one thing his genius brain couldn't do itself.

For about a year and a half (his junior and senior years of high school), he was in a recovery facility on the East Coast. He started with an emergency stay in an evaluative psychiatric facility and a temporary stint in a California rehab. He officially entered rehab on my mom's birthday, March 11, and she claims it was the best birthday gift she could ever have asked for. Her son, the most precious thing in her life, was finally taking the necessary steps to get the help he needed.

To me, who had watched Tyler get into trouble and experiment with substances for years, formally entering him into recovery felt like an acceptance of defeat—it was clear he would no longer naturally "grow out of it" or heed our pleas to stop. The problem was now a *thing*. My brother was officially an addict, not just a misbehaving kid. It seemed to me that acknowledging the situation in such a way gave it more power, solidified its reality. I resented this new reality but knew the alternative of not taking it seriously or hoping for the best was not a possibility any of us were willing to take.

What I remember most from my visit to Tyler in the initial psych ward was the intense strangeness of it all. It was bizarre seeing Tyler sitting in the beige bedroom with obscenities scratched into the walls, shoelaces confiscated from his sneakers. He seemed out of place among some of the other patients who screamed or cursed at us as we walked by, yet he did indeed fit the criteria required to be there. He seemed nonchalant about the whole thing, telling us stories of absurd things other kids had done and answering all my mom's questions about how he was doing. We gave him contraband snacks and then left him there, miles away from home, like he was at some horrible sleepaway camp. The divide between us as a family and him as an addict had silently nestled in between us and Tyler, and while we pledged to support him every step of the way, we knew there were many parts of this process he would now have to face alone.

We continued to visit him regularly when he was in the psychiatric facility across town. When he moved to a live-in facility in California for two months, mom and Jeff would fly out once every two weeks to see him. Finally, upon arriving at his long-term program back east, our parents would take flights and car trips to see him multiple times a month for the year he was there. While my family members had the flexibility to visit him, I was still in college or interning in San Francisco for a summer, so I did not see Tyler for over eight months at one point. The pain and anguish of missing him is second only to what I feel now. Even as I write this, it has not yet been eight months since I last saw him alive. Regardless, for the first time, we were all slightly relieved.

Someone else with actual addiction training was keeping a close eye on him while we had a bit of a break.

Through all his shuffling around from place to place, he still remained Tyler. His favorite counselor from his long-term facility, Dylan, described to me his first impression of Tyler when he finally arrived back on the East Coast for his yearlong stay. The staff took the patients on a wellness retreat in the woods and were doing an exercise together where each person went around the fire and shared stories about themselves when Tyler broke out into dance.

"Here was this kid, pale as can be, looked like he weighed a hundred pounds, with his shirt off for some reason," he recalled to me, barely containing laughter. "He started doing this interpretive dance, moving to the beat of people's words. At first it was hilarious, and then it became less funny as the joke was over and he kept doing it, until finally his commitment to the whole thing made it hilarious again."

Later in the retreat, my mom got a call from another counselor.

"Okay, first things first, Tyler is okay," he said into the phone, setting my mom's heart racing. She had gotten this phone call from a miscellany of authority figures too many times. The counselor then described an incident in which Tyler created a small hydrogen bomb and detonated it in the woods to the amusement of himself and the other campers. While this was technically not as serious an offense as a relapse, it was still not particularly encouraged.

These performances and similar antics, along with Tyler's gangly looks, earned him the nickname of Chicken Little. Rehab did not remove the intense joviality and goofy persona that my family and I had known and loved all his life. Dylan and the other counselors did not see it as completely positive, though. After probing him in therapy sessions for months, they began to realize that his commitment to entertaining was less of a fun, quirky personality trait and more of a distraction from being authentic or a symptom of the hyperactivity in his brain that did not let him sit still.

"There were moments when I wanted to just yell at him, 'Tyler, cut the shit,'" Dylan told me. He watched Tyler and saw how terrified he was of all the unknowns inside him. While he was extremely academically intelligent, his emotional intelligence was lacking, and he was often unable to express his feelings or even understand them. This emotional void was filled with any number of deflections. He was intensely guarded, and it took many months and attempts to break down the bullshit for Dylan and the other counselors to feel like they were making headway with Tyler.

While his intelligence and fearlessness were unique, they were not helpful, and they did not change the fact that underneath it all, he was still struggling with substance abuse just like the rest of his peers. His smarts meant that he was sneakier, studying for ingenious ways to work around the system, even more able to procure illicit substances because he knew things like which household chemicals he could use or combine to get himself high. His need for entertainment also had a daring, reckless side, and he did not have the instinct of danger or common sense that most of us have. Tyler was willing to push the boundaries and completely disregard safety, relying on his brains to get him out of any serious trouble.

His coping mechanisms were likewise unusual, yet just as unhelpful as the more textbook addict behavior. Instead of robbing a Target for drugs, Tyler did it for Legos, one of his favorite things to play with when he was bored, and his mind was racing. Instead of finding a dealer on the street, Tyler got drunk off the hand sanitizer and lemon Pledge that was used in his recovery house for cleaning. Either way, he was still avoiding his problems, getting caught, and pushing his recovery timeline back. He was funny and upbeat in front of others but always extremely damaging to himself.

Underneath all these erratic actions was, according to Dylan, a deep self-esteem problem and inability to handle negative emotions that were at the core of so many addicts' problems. Despite Tyler's one-of-a-kind personality, he was just like any other addicted person: in fact, Tyler's anxiety disorder and introduction to drugs at a young age made him more than twice as likely to develop an addiction problem as someone without these experiences (American Addiction Centers, 2020). The substance abuse was initially another coping mechanism, a symptom of his mental health struggles, but soon became its own beast. While Tyler exuded a daredevil confidence to the casual onlooker, his constant need to put on a show through humor or dangerous displays was really a quest for validation that he could not achieve organically within himself.

He also sought this validation with women, a department he was extremely successful in. His apparent confidence, whether real or manufactured, was attractive to many. Underlying problems aside, Tyler was always the life of the party, charismatic, funny, and good-looking (he does have my genes, after all). Chicken Little managed to hold two separate girlfriends while in rehab, and at some point during his stay, discovered that a third girl whom he had dated back home years before was also in the same program.

"How do you have another girlfriend? You are literally in *rehab!*" my mom yelled at him over the phone one day as I sat by and cried tears of hysterical laughter. Dating within the program was not necessarily banned but certainly frowned upon, especially in the earlier phases, in which patients' everyday activities are more heavily monitored.

While there were many similar bumps during his recovery journey, ultimately Tyler did make progress. Toward the end of his stay, Dylan and the other counselors noted that Tyler was beginning to mature and take the program more seriously than he had upon arrival. Partly a natural effect of growing up, partly a result of their repeated encouragement for him to get uncomfortable and try to talk through his pain, he was starting to show real improvement. For the first time, we all began to hope.

"Things just started to click for him," Dylan remembers. "He started to hold himself accountable, expressed more emotions, and understood that his actions had consequences. He was finally showing up."

The showboat disguise was finally cast aside, and Tyler thought more seriously about how his problems hurt his friends, family, and ultimately himself. When he got in trouble later toward the end of his stay for giving another patient information about how to get high, he was genuinely upset and contrite, a reaction completely unprecedented. When we visited Tyler around this time, he seemed focused on the future, determined to make it through the program and put this difficult chapter of his life behind him. My mom and dad smiled whenever they hung up the phone with him or one of his counselors, reassured of his positive momentum. We had finally broken through his bullshit and thought maybe things would actually be okay.

College posed the biggest problem for Tyler's recovery timeline. While his progress was encouraging, it was still fledgling and had not undergone any real tests of sobriety. He was not yet stable, and the counselors were not very comfortable with his ability to sustain his new coping skills and sobriety outside of the controlled recovery environment. Going from a sober living space to a college campus on the South Side of Chicago would be an enormous challenge for a newly sober addict. Yet Tyler, who had spent a year and a half away from his friends and family, constantly under surveillance and working through exhausting mental health struggles, was *begging* us to let him leave. He visited and put down a deposit at University of Illinois Chicago where he had been accepted as a chemical engineering major and fell in love with his new prospects. The thought of postponing his dreams was unbearable.

Our family was heavily divided on the subject. While we all wanted him to be as sturdy in his recovery as possible, there were two undeniable facts: Tyler did not want to be in rehab anymore, and he was now eighteen years old. We were unsure how he would react if we demanded that he stay and worried that he would leave prematurely of his own accord anyway. There was also the issue of motivation and the timeline of his life. He impressed us by completing his high school coursework virtually for the past year and a half, doing both schoolwork and the work of recovery at the same time. He took Advanced Placement and dual-enrollment college courses and graduated with honors to ensure his chances at going on to higher education stayed intact. Thus far, his long-term plan had not been disrupted. College, however, demanded a move to Chicago and a full-time academic commitment. He was beyond excited to go, as any high school senior would be, and it seemed cruel to deny him this next step, especially given how smart and passionate he was about chemistry and math. We did not want to postpone his new beginning at the risk of him losing all motivation or resenting us.

Ultimately, we made the decision to let him leave. He graduated from his recovery program and high school in the same month, constantly assuring us that he was ready, that he could do it. I remember sitting in my old high school gym watching him walk across the stage, hugging my mom as she cried tears of joy. It was the proudest moment of her life, and we truly began to let ourselves hope for the best. It was hard not to, watching that smiling face that we had seen experience such struggles, accepting a diploma that took him exponentially more effort than most kids to earn.

When Dylan got the phone call from my mom announcing his death, he was, like most of us, in shock.

"I still had the ghost peppers I confiscated from him in my desk," he said, a nod to another one of Tyler's publicity stunts. "We still talk about him all the time here; he was such a character."

Dylan was equally honored that my mom had thought to call him and tell him the news personally. It was a testament to Tyler's progress and the dedication of Dylan and the other staff members. Tyler, even in his most challenging days, talked about his support network with great respect and comradery. They took his death hard and took care of each other while cautiously disseminating the news throughout the patients who knew him and were still in the facility.

I had a sense of urgency to reach out to his rehab friends when Tyler died. Above all, I did not want them to think that Tyler had given up, hated his life, or saw no future. His death was an aberration during progress toward a sober life, not an abject failure of his own willpower. I wanted them to know that it was an accident, that he should still be a sign of hope for them, and they should remember him for how strong he was, and how he had every intention of fighting on, of getting control of his life back. His friends were all eager to speak to me, telling me stories of his kindness and humor, relieved to hear that he was happy and forward-thinking up until the moment of his death. My mom felt similarly, and even sent them a pizza party on the six-month anniversary of his death. She wrote a short speech for Dylan to deliver, sharing Tyler's story while encouraging them to keep fighting.

When I look at these other kids still struggling with their own journeys, I feel a strange mixture of jealousy and love. On the one hand, I think, *How the fuck do they still get to be alive, but Tyler doesn't?* It doesn't seem fair. There are others who have been addicted to hardcore substances like meth or opioids for years, have completely abandoned their recovery journeys or even their loved ones, or have otherwise caused a world of pain and destruction, yet are still managing to cling to life.

On the other hand, and with a much stronger force, after all this I only want the best for them. I can't bring Tyler back. What I can do is use his story and memory to help others. These kids loved and supported each other and stayed in contact after Tyler left for college, continuing to be his recovery cheerleaders even after he was on his own. I want these kids to remember Tyler for the sweet, genius, goofy kid that he was and use his legacy as a motivator in their own lives. While I am fortunate enough to not struggle with substance abuse myself, anyone can still appreciate how hard Tyler worked to try to stay clean. He was up against some pretty dark demons, and while he ultimately lost his battle, he never gave up. Tyler's fight acts as a model for my own battles, even though I will likely never face his specific struggles. If I can embody even an ounce of my brother's strength while I navigate my own hardships, I will be okay.

XI

———

Shortly after the funeral, my Aunt Pat took the time to go through old pictures of Tyler and me from childhood and digitize them, uploading them to a shared site for friends and family to see. These pictures were a complete novelty to me—when your parents are both remarried, you don't display many pictures from life in the previous marriage. Evidence of the first eleven years of my life was stored away tidily in storage boxes, making the post-funeral discovery an unexpected one.

These pictures triggered a phenomenon in me a few months after Tyler's death, when I realized that I was grieving two very different things. The first is obvious: I miss my brother as he was and want to cling to all the memories we shared together. The person he became in his nineteen short years on this Earth was loving, hilarious, and intelligent. I miss my best friend, the only person who was there with me through it all. The most fascinating part about those pictures was how they showed my relationship with Tyler as children. Sure, I miss Tyler as he was when he died, an adult with interests, hobbies, and a fully formed personality. Most of the memories we dwell on since his death concern him as teenager. I realized with those pictures how much I loved him when I was little. In every picture of the two of us, we are hugging or dancing or playing together—none of them are posed or forced. It occurred to me that I have always loved him, and he truly was there for every moment of my life.

While my mom and dad sent us back and forth between households, Tyler was by my side wherever I went. We were a package deal, and he helped make me into the person I am from the fundamental early days. When I look at that little girl laughing next to the baby brother she loves so much, I can't help but feel so sad for her. She has no idea she's going to lose it all one day. These pictures are a reminder that I lost more than I even thought. This first grief is deeper and more significant than I originally gave it credit for.

The second type of grief I experience is equally difficult but more complex. Not only did I lose Tyler as he was, but I also lost Tyler as he would have been, and I will continue to lose potential memories with him every single day. My wedding day will be missing a key groomsman, watching my other siblings graduate college will remind me of the loss, and I will have to raise children with no uncle.

So much grief is still left to be had, as I've realized every holiday or birthday that has happened since Tyler passed. Nothing reminds me of this more than when I talk to Olivia, Tyler's on-and-off girlfriend of five years. Sitting across from Olivia a month after Tyler died, I couldn't shake a feeling of unfairness: this girl should be my sister-in-law one day. There is an alternate universe in which Olivia and I spend every Christmas together, watching our kids play together around the tree. Now, she is just a girl who used to date Tyler, and the only way she will stay in my life is if we make an active effort to be friends.

Tyler and Olivia met their freshman year of high school on the anonymous imageboard website, 4chan. They were messaging each other, being silly and definitely not practicing internet safety, when they discovered they were the same age and lived within an hour of each other in northern Virginia. The two started talking relentlessly, sometimes staying on FaceTime with each other for twenty-four-hour stints. How Tyler convinced our mom that she was a real person and not a forty-year-old sex offender he met on the internet I will never know, but suddenly I was tasked with driving him the forty-five minutes to meet her at a movie theater in Berryville, Virginia. They went to see *Daddy's Home*, a true romance, on New Year's Day of 2016, and became boyfriend and girlfriend before I picked him up to drive home.

The two were obsessed with each other. They found a way to see each other despite the fact that they couldn't drive yet and lived an hour away from each other. They would go on dates to a mall in a good meeting place about halfway between them. They went to homecoming together and created their own language, and quite frankly annoyed the fuck out of the rest of us. On Valentine's Day, Tyler brought her flowers and wrote her a poem, and even spent one hundred dollars, an enormous sum for a fifteen-year-old, on her birthday gift. He dragged me to the outlet mall to help him pick out the perfect necklace for her, and we decided on a silver heart with a small amethyst in the center. He was so proud when he told the sales associate that he was getting a birthstone necklace for his girlfriend.

Telling me this story years later at the bagel shop table, Olivia began to laugh.

"You know my birthday's in June, right?" she said, and my hand flew to my mouth.

I am also born in June, so I realized immediately that Tyler had gotten her the wrong birthstone. June's stone is Alexandrite or pearl, while amethyst belongs to February. Olivia never told Tyler about his mistake, though, and kept the necklace no matter if they were together, broken up, fighting, or on good terms.

"I mean, it's so special," she explained to me. "I might get more pearl or Alexandrite jewelry one day, but no one will ever get me another amethyst."

They also did one thing that I will never forget, despite my best efforts. Whenever they were going down a flight of stairs together, they would desperately cling onto each other's arms and step down in sync, saying, "Chomp, chomp, chomp," with each step. A dorky but admittedly cute four-teen-year-old activity, they carried on doing it even when they got much older. Olivia explained it to me fondly and said that they would do it no matter where they were, no matter how inappropriate the occasion.

The two dated for a year and broke up for the first time and dated again briefly a few months later. Yet even when they were not together, they were still constantly in communication. They both dated other people but still talked every day (which, Olivia admitted, caused huge problems in her other relationships). When Tyler entered rehab his junior year of high school, he listed Olivia as one of his sober contacts, even though they had not been together for a while at that point. Despite their relationship status, the two were still each other's go-to source of emotional support.

Olivia knew about some of Tyler's issues. Even so, she was never confident that she knew the whole extent of the situation. At first, he hid it from her, and she pieced together a comprehensive summary through anecdotes and connecting certain events. He revealed some extremely concerning stories to her but discussed them like they were one-off events, and it was only through her own intuition that she realized there was a larger, ever-present issue at hand. She discouraged his drug use but was not personally affected by it very often. Tyler made sure to keep his drug problems separate from his relationship.

"I don't think he was ever fucked up around me, even during the worst times," she recalled. As a fifteen-year-old who never saw Tyler use drugs and who had no experience with drugs herself, it was hard for her to fully understand what was happening, and Tyler's problem remained separate, a thing outside of their perfect relationship.

Olivia also had her own problems, which only strengthened the bond she and Tyler shared. She went through an intense bout of traumatic incidents during that first year she was dating Tyler and fully credits him for taking care of her while she was at her most emotionally vulnerable. Indeed, I have seen level-headed, nonchalant Tyler truly angry and upset only once in my life: when a friend he introduced Olivia to was harassing her, saying terrible things to her about the aforementioned problems she faced.

"I'm going to fucking kill him," Tyler said, pacing back and forth around the room, wringing his hands. I was shocked and found it comical, seeing such a passive kid ready to initiate violence.

"Okay, buddy," I said. "You weigh, like, a buck twenty. You're not killing anybody."

"I wouldn't be alive today if it wasn't for Tyler," Olivia said to me, remembering how deeply she relied on this protective instinct.

The two of them had their entire life planned out together and would reference these plans even after they were broken up. They had their kids' names picked out (Wolfram and Valentina) and planned to go to the University of Virginia (my alma mater) and then move to North Carolina together. Tyler, who grew up in the suburbs of Washington, DC, was fascinated by Olivia's more rural life and wanted to live on a spacious farm in the South.

One day, Tyler came over to Olivia's house while her neighbors were on vacation. Their pigs had escaped from their pen and Tyler and Olivia had to chase them back in, a hilarious and completely foreign experience that Tyler absolutely loved. He would talk about those pigs all the time, and Olivia never had the heart to tell him that they went in for slaughter the next day.

As they got older, the plan didn't go quite as they wished—Tyler went into rehab, for one thing. Throughout his time there, Olivia stuck by his side as a friend, but it certainly made things difficult. The two were unable to see each other, and he missed their entire senior year. Tyler then chose to attend the University of Illinois Chicago while Olivia went to Virginia Tech. She kept trying to get him to transfer there. Unfortunately for her, he ended up really loving and finding a home at UIC and lost interest in transferring. Despite these hitches, the two remained steadfast in their belief that they would come back together one day after college.

The last time they saw each other was early in the summer Tyler died, after their first year at college. They started dating again, and Olivia came over to our house. To the rest of my siblings' and my annoyance, Mom let Olivia sleep over, breaking a rule she and Jeff were adamant about for the rest of us. Olivia was so happy about this, as Tyler had told her many times that one of his big dreams for them was to sleep together one day. Not in a sexual way, but he had a huge desire to fall asleep and wake up next to each other. Right before they went to bed, he turned on a song and the two slow danced since they never got the chance to attend prom together. The next day they said goodbye for the last time, unbeknownst to either of them.

About three months later on the morning of August 17, Olivia was back at college and woke up to go to work in a horrible mood. She called off and decided to drive the three hours from Virginia Tech back home, knowing she needed to be in a comfortable place even though she couldn't quite explain why. Five minutes after she walked into her parents' front door, my sister called her with the news of Tyler's death. She was devastated but also freaked out, wondering how she somehow knew to come home that day.

Another entirely bizarre event happened the day Olivia came up and ate bagels with me, about a month after Tyler's death. My mom had ordered several necklaces with Tyler's fingerprint engraved on them, one for each family member and his closest friends. Olivia made the list, and the necklaces were delivered that same morning. Her laptop stopped working, forcing her to drive back to Northern Virginia to get a replacement from home, as she had urgent schoolwork to complete. As the necklaces were arriving at our house and she was leaving her apartment, her amethyst necklace snapped off its chain. Tyler's amethyst necklace *that she had been wearing for almost five years* broke the very morning that both the new necklaces arrived, and she had to return to the area.

She immediately set up lunch with me, and we had a wonderful day together. My mom gave her the new necklace, we had our bagels, and then sat in his room for a few hours reminiscing. I will never forget the indescribable feeling of lying on Tyler's carpet among his dirty socks, staring at my would-be, should-be sister-in-law, wishing so badly that she would be part of my family one day. I even told my step-brother after he left that it was his job to marry her now, though he didn't much take to the idea.

I always took it for granted that Olivia would be in my life forever. We were never terribly close ourselves, but I always had so much love for her because of what she meant to Tyler. I saw the way he looked at her, the way he cared about her, like he never cared for anyone. There are so many things Tyler will never get to do, but he did get to experience true love before he died, something not even I have felt yet. And while I can't watch him grow up, I can watch this girl who was so fundamentally changed and helped by him grow up, find love once more, and hopefully start a family with better-named children. I want to see the girl Tyler taught to love use that love to make a beautiful life for herself.

That day on Tyler's floor, bellies full of bagels, Olivia and I made a pact to stay in each other's lives forever. I will be at her wedding, though it's not the one I hoped for, and she will be at mine. She will help to fill the emptiness that Tyler left behind, to make this loss of possibility a little more bearable. To me, she is part of Tyler, and he is part of her. He is gone, but I can still hold on to this real, tangible part of him that he loved more than anything. The two are the definition of twin flames, each a half of the other's soul, and I want to see this half grow up and thrive despite missing the other.

On the way home from our house that day, Olivia was crying in the car. While our day was meaningful and positive, as soon as she left, she was overwhelmed with missing Tyler.

At some point flying down I-81 she shouted out, "Give me a sign!" and as soon as the words left her mouth, her entire radio system shut off, and displayed an error message that was not even listed in the user's manual. Since that day, Olivia has lost two more laptops. And while she is not fond of the particular signs that Tyler has chosen, she is grateful to still feel the presence of her twin flame, her "what if," watching over her as she moves toward the future she deserves.

XII

Olivia and Tyler were not together when he died—they remained close friends as they always had, but Tyler was seeing someone else at the end, a girl he knew from high school named Stella. Their relationship was long and complicated, so I asked Stella to sit down with me after he passed and help me piece together their timeline.

The two met when he was a junior in high school, she a freshman. They had study hall together and quickly became close, texting and sneaking out to listen to music together or make out as high schoolers do. Tyler once even walked all the way from our mom's house to Stella's, easily two and a half miles, in the middle of the night while on drugs. Stella was going through an experimental phase of her own during that time, not doing anything nearly as extreme as Tyler, yet curious enough to find his tales of nights on MDMA and psychedelic mushrooms intriguing. He was older, could drive, and had a bad boy persona. He showed a softer side as well, writing her poems and telling her he loved her, but Stella's own personal life and circumstances prevented them from dating. Tyler went to his first recovery facility during the height of the first half of their relationship, and the two fell out of touch.

When COVID-19 struck and Tyler landed back in Leesburg, Stella took the opportunity to check in on her old
friend. She had been thinking about him, wondering how
he was doing since rehab, and finally reached out to him via
Instagram in the midst of her quarantine boredom. They
quickly rekindled their previous friendship, and things once
again turned romantic. She would come over to "watch a
movie" while my mom and stepdad rolled their eyes. As time
went on, the couple took a step back and worked backward,
getting less physical and more friendly. They began spending
almost every day together and often included Stella's best
friend Yvonne in their outings. The three would drive around
listening to music or spending time outside.

By the end of July, Stella's romantic feelings for Tyler
surfaced once more, and Tyler decided to officially ask her
to be his girlfriend. She came to our house, and he panicked because he wanted to get her flowers and didn't have
time—instead, he drew a picture of some flowers on a piece
of notebook paper torn from one of his school notebooks and
popped the question. Stella denied him and instead requested
they take things slowly and not attach a label, to which Tyler
reluctantly agreed. She then went on a mini vacation to Virginia Beach for Yvonne's birthday, and called him while tipsy.

"Hey, Tyler," she giggled over the phone. "I love you."

"I love you too," he laughed back. She describes this
moment as more of a display of genuine affection rather than
a big romantic declaration. Regardless of its intention, it was
meaningful to both, and Tyler was genuine in his words. The
up-and-down nature of their relationship never shook the
foundation of mutual care.

The day before he died, a Sunday, the two went on a hike.
Tyler was notoriously an indoor kid, so we were all impressed

at this girl's ability to get him to step foot in the woods, and we knew he must really like her. However, that evening, he told our mom that she had seemed off the whole day, and Tyler immediately guessed at the possible cause. The two finished the hike and parted ways so Tyler could pick up my mom and stepdad from the airport, and the truth was uncovered once they started texting. Stella said she was still handling some personal issues and didn't feel ready to jump in the way he did, so they left each other in a bit of an awkward standstill.

Tyler seemed distraught when he picked up my mom and stepdad and went to bed early. He told my mom briefly about his troubles, saying that he was bummed but would work it out with her in the morning. He said goodnight to the family, and after my mom left him, he and Stella texted for a while and promised to see each other the next day to talk things through.

The entire time they were together, Tyler fooled Stella just as he fooled us, but he was a little more honest with her about the extent of his relapses. He would drive immediately from an innocent hang out with her and Yvonne to a pill run with another friend, Kyle, never missing a beat. Stella did not like or trust Kyle at all and was surprised when I told her the two had been spending so much time together. While Tyler told Stella about a few instances of his drinking or taking pills, he always sounded remorseful, like it was a one-off mistake, not as if it were a common habit weaving through his entire summer experience. He kept that part of himself mostly separate from her and never led on that it was anything more than a few slipups. In that way, the two continued their peaceful coexistence, and Stella never felt particularly anxious about his safety or well-being.

This is hard to comprehend for me, who would have a full-on panic attack whenever I found out that Tyler had drank a few beers. Nevertheless, I have to remind myself that not everyone was part of Tyler's worst days, the time right before and during rehab, when his existence itself was touch-and-go. Just like his college friends, Stella was not present for the nightmare that wreaked havoc on our family for years, so a confession of his drinking or taking a few pills was not perceived as a red alert, a sign that he was once again spiraling out of control.

When I stepped off the five-hour flight at Dulles International Airport the night of August 17, I checked my Instagram account and had a message from Stella, who at that point I had only met once in passing.

"Hey! This is Stella, I'm a friend of Tyler's. He hasn't been responding to me and I was just wondering if you knew if he was okay? Or if you could give me you guys' mom's number."

My stomach sank. The two had plans to meet again that day and talk things over after the hike, but Tyler never showed. I immediately called around to see if someone had told her already. My younger sister, Courtney, had already broken the news to her. Thinking about the situation crushed me. How many times have I not heard from someone for a few hours and wondered what was wrong? In every case it was either a dead phone, a lack of signal, or a change of plans. Stella was fully expecting Tyler to reemerge from oversleeping or forgetting his phone somewhere and was wholly unprepared for this, the absolute worst-case scenario.

After processing the initial shock, Stella was wracked with guilt as we all were. Her guilt was exacerbated: she was one of, if not the very last person to speak to Tyler, and after more details of his death became known, it was clear that Tyler took the pill that killed him directly after saying goodnight to her. How could she not feel guilty, wondering if he was so upset by her change of heart that he accidentally poisoned himself? We all feel guilty for various reasons (Did we do enough? Should we have checked on him one last time? Should we have put him back in rehab at the first sign of trouble instead of trusting him to get better?), but Stella undoubtedly had it the worst. At only seventeen years old, she had to wrestle with the idea, however untrue, of being the cause of Tyler's death.

It took many reassurances from our family to make her finally believe that no, Tyler's death was not her fault, nor any single person's. He suffered from addiction and substance abuse issues for years and had already purchased the pill before he went on the hike with Stella the day before his death. Had she not hurt his feelings that night, he may very well have still taken it for fun or taken it the next day because something else stressed him out. We knew that Tyler's brain was always working, his hyperactivity always causing an overwhelming anxiety. His entire life was a constant battle that began long before he even knew Stella existed. It could easily have happened any of the hundreds of times he took an illicit substance. In fact, we were lucky that he made it to nineteen. For lack of a better way to phrase it, it was bound to happen with or without Stella's influence. At some point after almost a decade of fraternizing with dangerous substances, Tyler's luck finally ran out. Stella's role in his death was purely circumstantial, but that hardly makes it more comforting.

Since he passed, she has spent a lot of time with my mom and me (my mom even gets a coffee at the restaurant where Stella works several times a week after her morning run). When I was finally ready to hear it, she agreed to explain the details of their relationship, details I would never have known or cared about had Tyler still been alive. His death transformed her in my eyes from the girl my little brother had around to one of the last and most meaningful relationships he had before he passed, and the more I hear about their friendship, the more thankful I am to her for making his last few months memorable and filled with a simple happiness removed from the drugs.

Stella has been a critical part of my family's own healing process, especially my mom's. Regardless of the romantic complications the two of them had, her love and care for my brother is wildly apparent. She visits his grave almost every day, cleans it up and decorates it during seasonal changes, and has even declared to read him this book out loud once it is completed (Hi, Tyler!). She, my mom, and I rely on each other to remind us of how Tyler's presence lives on. Stella has come over for dinner and performed some of Tyler's favorite songs at our town's monthly outdoor musical event. Her continued efforts to remember and celebrate him come purely from the heart, and I can tell she genuinely misses him.

Stella is a perfect example of what I consider the Tyler effect, his ability to form a completely unique and meaningful relationship with everyone he met. In the weeks after his death, my social media inboxes were flooded with messages from people I had never even heard of sharing stories of his kindness and charm. Two of his classmates at college, neither of whom I had ever met, even sent me letters. One detailed how he had walked one of them home from a party and spent the night telling stories and pigging out on junk food instead of drinking with the rest of the group. The other described how smart and willing to help others with their homework he was. He made such an impression on everyone he met, and each person had their own, completely special relationship with him. Stella had her own, and while I never paid her much attention as one of Tyler's love interests, I now saw Tyler's beautiful love for people that she represented.

There was a single hilarious moment at his funeral when a string of seven or eight ex-girlfriends filed into our backyard for the post-service reception. They were all gorgeous, each way out of Tyler's league, and each one sniffling into their sleeve or offering condolences to the family. Each girl delivered a touching speech to my mom about how special Tyler had been to them—whether a brief fling in middle school or a long-term affair like Olivia, each one told stories about his exceptional thoughtfulness and care. He wrote love letters, bought flowers, and made a big display of asking for a date to homecoming.

He was not a player. He did truly care about each of these girls in completely different ways, and his displays of affection were genuine. I took his goofy, carefree persona at face value. I knew he had girlfriends, but I never paid much attention longer than it took me to roll my eyes. I was wary of a teenage boy's capacity for emotional depth, especially ones who set off water bottle bombs in the backyard and snuck girls into the basement. Little did I know that for Tyler, no two relationships were alike, and only after his death did I discover the actual emotional complexity of my baby brother; the same person I have a video of rolling a condom over his entire head and face.

We think Tyler still visits some of these most special relationships posthumously in the form of butterflies. While it sounds crazy, it's one of those things that has happened too many times and in too strange of circumstances to ignore. It started as a joke when I found a big, yellow butterfly on the porch the night after Tyler's funeral. My mom and I were exhausted, and I used it as an excuse to drag her away from the lingering crowd of family and friends.

"Look, Mom," I smiled and put an arm around her. "A yellow butterfly. Tyler's favorite color."

Tyler, who was woefully colorblind, decided at a young age that yellow was his favorite since it was the color of Sponge-Bob. We declared this butterfly a sign from him, but the next day discovered that it was fake, a paper ornament that fell off one of the flower displays—not a living creature sent down from the heavens. Things started to get weird, though. We started seeing yellow butterflies *everywhere*, sometimes at the most crucial times. There have been moments when my mom or I will literally ask Tyler for a butterfly, and one will immediately present itself, as if to say, "Hi guys! I'm listening."

We told Stella about the butterfly phenomenon, to which she nodded politely. She did not believe in the butterflies herself until she was installing some flowerpots at his gravesite and an enormous yellow butterfly (this one real) immediately landed right on the plant she had just potted. Similar-looking butterflies have appeared to me, my mom, Stella, and some of our other friends and family just at the moment we need a sign from Tyler.

I don't claim to know if signs from the dead are real or not, but at some point, you have to find something to believe. If looking for butterflies makes my brother's untimely death just a tiny bit more bearable, I'm running with it. Some of the circumstances seem too timely to be coincidences, so I question them no further.

Stella asked me about the butterflies while writing her college essay. In the tradition of undergraduate essay prompts encouraging you to revisit your worst traumas, she wanted to write about Tyler and the way she came to believe in the butterflies. She had some reservations about choosing the topic as she didn't want to take advantage of the situation or be insensitive to the tragedy. I struggled with the same thoughts when writing my own applications for graduate programs and wrestled with feelings of using my brother's death for my own personal gain until I voiced this concern with one of my professors.

"You're worried about taking advantage of the trauma, but...was it *not* extremely traumatizing? Was it *not* a huge piece of adversity you had to overcome?" she reminded me. "You're not milking anything. Your brother *did* in fact die, and it did change your life in an extreme and horrible way. That's the whole point. You're surviving it, so claim it."

I gave Stella my full blessing to write about the butterflies, and it got her an acceptance into the honors college at the school of her choice.

The negative ramifications of Tyler's death are obvious, but there is room to accept and discover positive ones as well. For instance, we created a memorial fund in his name to support mental health and addiction that already has tens of thousands of dollars in it. Tyler's death helped me rekindle and strengthen some of my own relationships as people reached out to offer their support. If our resilience in the wake of Tyler's death proves to various admissions committees how strong Stella's and my characters are, so be it. It's not a lie, and I believe stating the truth about what you've been through is not taking advantage. Part of remembering the one you lost is being honest about what happened, both the good parts and the bad. It has and will continue to shape Stella's and my lives forever, and it's okay to claim that.

I want Tyler to be a part of everything I do until the day I also leave this Earth. I want as many positive events to ripple from both his life and death as possible. Maybe the memorial fund will help save someone's life, or one of my rekindled relationships will turn out to be my future husband, or Tyler's story will help Stella and me get into our dream schools. What happened to him is unchangeable, but through her active remembrance and claiming of the experience, Stella taught me that we must make the best of what we are given. I prefer to remember Tyler in as happy a way as possible and find as many reasons as I can to thank him. Since he can't share the experience of watching me get into grad school or getting married here on Earth, I hope that his legacy intertwines itself with all these life events so that I can keep him with me no matter what I do. I have full confidence that he will be a part of our lives, no matter where he is.

XIII

———

Tyler met his best friend in middle school. Dean was a new kid who had just moved to Virginia and spent most of his seventh-grade year in an awkward preteen solitude. I remember how weird and uncomfortable middle school was for me, and I had the head start of going to the feeder elementary school. I can't imagine going through it as a brand-new face, having puberty's awfulness run up against moving to a new state loneliness. Nevertheless, by eighth grade, Dean began to branch out and met Tyler in their technical education class.

At this point, Tyler was known around school as a kid who had "done stuff." In eighth grade, "stuff" mostly meant sneaking alcohol and trying weed, but it still gave him a bad boy reputation. Dean describes the period of his life when he met Tyler as "depressing," so he was intrigued by the new possibility of using substances to quell his adolescent ennui. The two struck up a friendship and immediately realized they had more in common than their itch to experiment with drugs. The two were smart beyond their years, and a menace to the teachers in their advanced math classes.

"We were such little fucks," Dean told me over a FaceTime call.

Indeed, Tyler's high school math teacher I talked with told me the same thing in kinder terms, using "annoying" and "energetic" in place of expletives. Their time in the classroom was equal parts intense curiosity about math and talking or goofing around at inappropriate times. It seemed all their intelligence was based in incredible academic skills, leaving their emotional intelligence and maturity in the dust. The two of them didn't have many intellectual equals in their lives, so a natural companionship formed quickly.

They were best friends, yet my parents did not like Tyler hanging out with Dean, and Dean's parents did not like him hanging out with Tyler. I got my driver's license just at the start of Dean and Tyler's eighth-grade year, meaning I was on the hook for driving Tyler to Dean's or taking Dean home from our house. Each time Tyler would ask to hang out, my mom or dad would begrudgingly accept, extremely nervous but ultimately realizing that Tyler had been getting into trouble long before he met Dean—he was not being corrupted by his influence. In fact, it was often most likely the other way around.

The two got in trouble a handful of times, most notably when they were caught smoking weed in our basement. In the single least sneaky act of rebellion I had ever seen, the two started smoking in the *windowless basement storage room*, somehow not noticing that they were smelling up the entire house. It was also for reasons like this that our parents let the friendship continue; the immaturity, or sometimes simple stupidity, of their misdemeanors made it seem like they would just grow out of it. Our older stepbrother, Connor, had also been caught sneaking weed and alcohol in middle school, and he indeed matured and now leads a life free of any addiction. Dean ended up following in Connor's footsteps, largely sticking with social drinking or smoking through high school, trying more exotic drugs like mushrooms or ecstasy once in a blue moon, but never having it become a real problem in his life.

Tyler was different. He was exploring harder drugs like meth in early high school and using substances more frequently, oftentimes alone. It was not a social enhancement for him. Instead, it was a concerning pattern. While Dean remained his best friend, the two became less able to connect as Tyler's habits became more intense, their common ground of misbehaving boyhood evaporating. By the beginning of junior year, Tyler seemed to be getting in trouble virtually every day, each time more seriously. Things finally came to a head when Dean called me one day in a panic.

"Hi Alexis," he stammered nervously. "I don't want to be a snitch, but…I'm really worried. Check your phone."

I did, and what I saw horrified me. There on my screen was a picture texted to me by Dean of my baby brother's arm, punctured next to a used needle. I lost it.

To this day, I credit Dean for saving Tyler's life. Tyler could very well have died a lot sooner had Dean not broken the teenage golden rule and tattled on him. Looking at that picture was the first time that I truly began to accept Tyler's actions as more than something you just grow out of, and I knew that just like Dean, it was imperative that I break Tyler's confidence and tell someone who could help. I showed my mom, who was equally horrified, and thus began the process of confrontation and moving Tyler to a recovery facility.

Dean was sad to watch his best friend enter rehab, finding the gap between them widening even further. While Tyler was not angry with Dean for telling on him, it was clear that their childhood antics were a thing of the past, Dean now a "normal" high schooler occasionally partying, Tyler a kid whose entire life was out of control. The two stayed in touch and Dean continued to support him, talking less often but still always worrying about his recovery.

Tyler came home for Christmas that winter, taking the train from New England down to Union Station in Washington, DC. Even though it was an hour's drive into the city, I was so excited to see him that I offered to pick him up.

"Can I come with you?" Dean asked as soon as I told him my plan.

The two had been talking about hanging out when Tyler was back in town. I hadn't realized just how much they missed each other until Dean and I began our drive. He rode along with me in nervous excitement the whole way, asking me questions about what Tyler was like when I had seen him in rehab, how he was doing. By the time we arrived, the two of us were practically bouncing off the walls, anxiously glancing around the lobby of the train station to see if Tyler was coming.

When he finally arrived, he was just as excited as Dean. I bought them an overpriced lunch from one of the station restaurants and sat back while the two of them chatted away, making up for all the lost time. Tyler seemed so normal, and I could tell Dean was thinking the same thing and was probably relieved. His best friend, for all his struggles, was still his best friend.

Months later, I took a picture of the two of them in front of my old high school, caps and gowns in tow. Graduation was a moment none of us ever thought of as a given, and there was a sense that day that maybe things were finally returning to normal for Tyler. I wonder if Dean felt it too, thinking maybe Tyler would still turn out like he and Connor did, with a mischievous childhood behind him but a bright future ahead. The two spent time together that summer and left for their respective colleges in August. Despite all the hurdles, the two boys were on the same path once more.

Dean thought Tyler was staying sober in college, just like we did. Right before the two left for their separate universities, Dean even called Tyler to come pick him up, trashed, from a party. Tyler obliged and handled the situation with nonchalance, neither relapsing nor judging Dean for his actions. We were all impressed and took it as a good sign that Tyler could be around people partying without falling off the wagon. Every text or visit during breaks reassured Dean that his friend was living the same college life that he was. They would hang out and talk about their own fun experiences and challenges at school, regaining some of the lost common ground. Before he found his stride in Chicago, Tyler even considered transferring to the school where Dean went.

Then, when COVID-19 struck and the two were back in the same town, they spent even more time together in person. The same months where Tyler was lying to Stella and sneaking around with some new, suspicious friends, he was also riding bikes with Dean. There is a common thread between the important people in Tyler's life, the ones who had his best interests at heart and cared for his well-being more than they wanted to have a good time: they all exposed him to the outdoors. Tyler was by nature an indoors kid, always up to speed on the latest Xbox release or finding a new movie universe to be obsessed with (*Star Wars* and Quentin Tarantino films were among the most annoying). With Olivia and her farm life, Stella and her hikes, and Dean and his bike rides all pushing Tyler out of his comfort zone, each one forced him to try new things that he always enjoyed but would never do of his own accord.

Dean describes these bike rides and the last summer in general as pure, innocent fun. The two would ride for a few miles on the Washington & Old Dominion Trail, Tyler would get excited whenever he saw cows, and they would return for lunch, Tyler smiling and sunburnt. His wholesome activities with Stella and Dean, while genuine, reassured us that he was doing well and maintaining healthy social relationships, while distracting us from the fact that he was using drugs again.

Dean now realizes that he, like the rest of us, was really just entertaining a fantasy that summer. Tyler was acting normal, getting his summer schoolwork done, holding a job, and spending time with his good friends, lulling us all into a false sense of security. A few times Dean even put time with Tyler off, whether to go to a party with a different group of friends or simply because he was busy. Neither boy had a particular sense of urgency if they couldn't spend as much time together as they wanted, feeling as if their friendship had already endured so much, they were solid.

"I just thought he would be there forever," Dean told me shortly after acting as one of Tyler's pallbearers.

Like me, he experienced the immediate guilt that comes with death, where you reevaluate your entire relationship with the deceased, overanalyzing every interaction and non-interaction, wondering if that person really did know that you cared about them. I have been watching Dean cope since Tyler's death, frequently worrying about him as I am with everyone who was close with my brother. Just like Olivia, I absolutely do not want Tyler's death to mean the relationship Dean has with me and my family is gone. Also, like

Olivia, Dean was hit extremely hard by the loss of Tyler, yet he does not have the support network I do—the rest of his family is not mourning beside him, he did not receive dozens of flower bouquets, and most people in his life simply never knew Tyler.

Dean and I talk several times a week at least and stay up to speed on the major points of each other's lives. We both turn to each other when needed and are planning a celebration for Tyler for his first birthday since he passed. Dean is embracing this loss, not running from it, and keeping his best friend close. We both carry him with us as we go and keep him present partly by this continuation of our own relationship with each other.

Every time we speak, Dean reassures me that he is doing just fine that he has a support network in place and feels emotionally taken care of. In fact, he has taken one of the most inspiring approaches to handling Tyler's death of anyone I know.

"I check on people more," he explained to me. "I look out for my friends and try harder if I know they're struggling. I just want to help people."

In the same way that I want to claim and celebrate all the positive aftermath of Tyler's death, Dean has used it as a motivation to be a better person, a better friend. Most of the ways I have been able to healthily deal with grief are similar to this, turning a bad emotion (like guilt for not hanging out with your best friend more often the summer before he died) and turning it into a positive force going forward (being an advocate for mental health and committing to looking after those he cares about). While Dean is still devastated, I can tell that he is making every effort to continue Tyler's legacy and do as much good as possible in his honor. While I still sometimes see him as my annoying little brother's annoying best friend, I also notice the maturity and care he now possesses. He is both in touch with his own emotions while expressing empathy toward others. He learned a valuable lesson from losing his best friend and is using it to better himself and the world.

I write for the same reason, not to make some futile attempt to bring Tyler back, but to move forward and help those who can still be helped. Whenever I feel like all I am doing is worthless, I remember Dean's mission and all the other Tylers out there who could still use a best friend looking out for them.

XIV

As I mentioned, one of the best parts about life after Tyler's death is learning new things about him. However, this can also be the worst. Some things are truly beautiful, stories of the kindness and dependability he gave freely. One girl who was in rehab with him told me that Tyler took a two-hour bus ride with her so that he could be there for moral support as she had blood tests done, just because she was scared of needles. Another rehab friend told me that one day he used the last money in his checking account to buy them Chinese food. A college friend said that one night at a party he wanted to leave, and Tyler was the only one who agreed to end his night early and accompany him back to the dorms, where they enjoyed a night in, pigging out on snacks. Tyler had this incredible ability to be there for you when you needed him and hearing these stories after his death reaffirmed for me that he was a good person, for whatever that's worth. He would drop everything, even his own responsibilities, when someone he cared about needed a favor or just wanted company.

Some of the stories are not nearly as pleasant, however. We learned about secret relapses and got more context around suspicious situations, confirming our biggest fears.

Some things I've learned about Tyler have completely broken my heart. Immediately after his death, I had no sense of guilt or an idea that I could have done something to stop his death. This changed after several friends filled in some of the unknowns about his life in college, away from our family. Uncovering the truth that he was still using drugs, I struggled with feeling like we could have saved him or at least could have done more to help. I try to tell myself that, no, Tyler was an excellent liar, and the fact that these stories surprise me so much means there was no way I could have known, but was I just not looking hard enough on purpose? Did I, and the rest of my family, choose to not see what we didn't want to see? Did we naively believe that Tyler was really better so we could sleep at night?

The most relatable account of this guilt I have ever read is David Sheff's detail in *Beautiful Boy* of his son Nic's addiction. He grapples with both the incessant paranoia of loving someone with addiction that is paired with the need for reassurance. In one scene where Nic swears he is sober, David states, "With practice, addicts become flawlessly gifted liars, and this coincides with parents' increasing susceptibility to their lies. I believed Nic because I wanted to believe him—I was so desperate to believe him." This is how I felt about Tyler, to the letter.

I never knew exactly what my role in Tyler's recovery should be. I was not his parent, so I could not make any decisions for him, but I was also extremely involved in the entire saga, and it certainly weighed heavily on my consciousness. When I would try to express my opinions, my voice was never considered over those of my parents, the doctors, and the counselors. I sometimes feel like I did not voice my concerns enough, then I laugh—to think that my parents were not equally or even more anxious than I was is completely absurd. To quote David Sheff again, "Parents of addicts don't sleep."

At some point during his substance abuse issues, Tyler (and Nic) became an adult, becoming more cunning just as my parents lost the ability to legally control his actions. He graduated from both his rehab program and high school and was accepted into the University of Illinois Chicago. He seemed to have turned a real corner and assured us that he was ready to be out in the world on his own. He was also adamant that he did not want to go back to treatment, and we couldn't force him to. Our choices were to accept his statement of sobriety and support his dreams of going to college or fight against his wishes and risk him abandoning or hating us.

The night he relapsed at the Christmas party, I remember him telling our mom that it was fine that all the relatives were drinking; he was in college now and was exposed to drugs and alcohol all the time but had yet to succumb to temptation. After he died, I asked his college friend, Carmen, if he was actually sober. She looked at me with a pitiful knowledge written on her face and said, "Yeah...for like, four days."

Carmen and his college roommate, Avery, shared with me a startling truth: Tyler was consistently fucked up for the majority of his time at college. He smoked marijuana almost every day and became known as a stoner, letting hallmates smoke from his "gravity bong." Carmen said he did many other things as well, some as tame as drinking, others as severe as making meth in the abandoned dorm buildings across campus. When I asked how their friend group felt about this, she stated that they simply told him to not bring it back to their room. This was completely new and shocking information to me—I felt my entire perception of Tyler's last year of life crashing down around me.

Carmen filled in some of the context of incidents our family *did* already know about as well. Tyler hurt his foot one weekend and made up a fake story to tell our mom, saying he accidentally hit it on a chair. Carmen told me that he was actually on a bender the entire weekend, completely fucked up on a dangerous mixture of alcohol and Xanax. In his drug-induced fog he trashed the room, breaking one of the bathroom sinks, stole weed and alcohol from a couple different people in the hall, then passed out. When his friends realized he had stolen from them, they went to confront him in his room, waking him from his drug-induced slumber. This angry, abrupt wake-up reminded him of a time he was jumped while in rehab, and since he was still fucked up and felt awful for what his bender had caused, he spiraled into a full-blown panic attack. At this point, he broke his foot while smashing his roommate's dresser with his own chair. Carmen had to calm him down and stayed up all night waiting for him while other hallmates took him to the hospital for his foot.

Panic attacks were common for Tyler, and we were told that *another* of them had caused him to accidentally hurt himself to the point that he landed in the hospital. Apparently, he had taken painkillers that were prescribed for the previous broken foot incident. How the emergency room doctor didn't look into his medical history and see that he was absolutely not allowed to take painkillers, I have no idea. He took more than his prescription recommended and was once again belligerently high. Afterward, Tyler went into a Walgreens and began stealing things off the shelves at random, not even attempting to hide them or sneak away from employees. The security guards at the door quickly accosted him, and when Tyler realized he was about to be arrested, he *pretended* to have a panic attack. Thinking he was mentally unstable, the security guards sent him to the hospital rather than calling the police. Upon arriving back at the dorm, his friends were impressed at his ability to narrowly avoid an arrest.

As Carmen told me these stories, my heart sank. I asked her at one point if they were ever genuinely concerned for Tyler's well-being, and she told me about a running joke the group had: if Tyler was too messed up, someone would say, "Get him out of here. I don't want him dying in *my* room." She even told me that the day before he died, he mentioned opioids to the group. They reprimanded him, saying they would not allow anything stronger than weed or alcohol into their shared apartment the next school year. Carmen made plans to buy Narcan just in case.

By the end of this conversation with Carmen, I was fucking furious. How could all these people know about Tyler's substance abuse issues, know that he was in rehab for almost two years, and watch him spiral out without ever saying a word? They were all eighteen or nineteen years old, but even Tyler's sixteen-year-old best friend in high school knew to alert me when he started shooting up speed in the school bathrooms. I couldn't believe that no one, not a single person in the friend group, thought to mention his constant relapsing to anyone in our family. Then to see this girl sitting there, telling me about how she used to chase him around the dorm halls when he was high and running loose. It sounded like she didn't understand the severity of the situation, and now he was dead. I looked at her, wondering, *How can you sleep at night?*

I hung up the phone with her and immediately called my mom, practically screaming obscenities on the phone. She was equally angry, and the two of us bonded in our contempt for those who knew he was in trouble but did nothing to stop it.

This feeling eventually passed as my own guilt came and went. Tyler was halfway across the country from both me and my mom, with plenty of time and privacy to do drugs without us ever knowing. That fact assuaged me of my own guilt, but David Sheff's story still haunted me and made me realize that the responsibility for keeping the addicted person sober is more complicated than one person's choices. Even if Tyler was getting fucked up in my mom's house, would she, would I, would any of us have let ourselves believe that he was in serious trouble? Would we have even known? Had he not relapsed twice in front of us, and still found a way to convince us that he was fine? Relapsing is a natural part of recovery, after all (Sack, 2012). No one is perfect and having a bad relapse with drugs can reinforce the need for sobriety. Who's to say that we would have done any better than his friends, especially since Tyler was so averse to going back to rehab?

For Tyler's first birthday since he passed, we threw a party with family and friends, and Carmen and Avery came. Spending more time with them also made me realize a few things. First, these kids were Tyler's friends, not his parents. Avery often pleaded with Tyler to stop or told him the drugs made him uncomfortable, and once even went so far as to lock all Tyler's drugs in a cabinet with a bike lock. His efforts could not entirely stop Tyler, though—he was a legal adult making his own decisions and knew how to be sneaky when his friends tried to step in his way. They also knew the deal my mom had made with Tyler, that if he showed signs of relapsing or getting bad grades, he would have to drop out of school. This was his last chance, so tattling on him would mean losing their best friend. Avery recalled a time when he declared his intentions to call our mom until Tyler literally begged him not to, and he put the phone down when he realized it would mean the end of their friendship and his time at school. Carmen told me, "To this day, I go back and forth, feeling guilty for not telling you sooner and feeling guilty for telling you at all."

A second realization lightened my anger even further: they had no context for Tyler's addiction when they met him. Sure, they knew he used hard substances. Carmen even described Tyler as a "tank," always bragging about how much he could do and how much control he had. What they didn't know was how awful it was to sit by his side in a hospital bed, to cry on the phone listening to the rehab counselor tell us he was drinking household chemicals, or to embark on the six-hour car rides up to Connecticut just so we could have our entire family together on Christmas. To college kids who are experimenting with drugs and alcohol for the first time themselves, they might not have understood the seriousness of the substances Tyler was doing, either. Had I not tried a few party drugs during my own college tenure, had some crazy nights, done some stupid things? There he was, after all, an upper-middle class suburban kid still attending college and keeping his life together—I don't think he fit anyone's mental schema of an addict in danger.

These kids took Tyler's death extremely hard, convincing me of their ignorance of the situation's direness. His room-mate, Avery, didn't tell us that Tyler was relapsing, but after his death he was barely able to eat and considered dropping out of school. He saw Tyler as just another first-year college student like himself, partying it up, not as an actual threat to himself. When the end came, he was floored. He flew in from Chicago to be a pallbearer and barely said a word the whole time he was there. Talking to him a few months later, when he had a little more time to process, his words broke my heart.

"I didn't believe it at first," Avery told me. "We would mostly just smoke weed together, and whenever he did anything else, we could rein him in before he went too out of control. Like if he tried to leave the room at 3:00 a.m. to go do some drug, we'd stop him and make him go back to bed. It all seemed normal, just a college thing. When they told me he died, it didn't make sense to me. Then it kind of settled in, but it was so weird. I was living in this apartment, and it was really hard to see his empty room every day. Now I'm a little more used to it, but it's still just this huge thing I have to live with."

I also shifted my focus to the other parts of Carmen's stories, the parts about her and Avery taking care of Tyler when he was on drugs. Her corralling him in the hallways was just one of the many things she did to keep him safe. She said she would talk him out of doing more serious drugs, make sure he did not take dangerous pills while already drunk, and stay with him if he was starting to panic. While she failed to notice or tell anyone that he was relapsing and in need of help, how many times did she save his life? Based on the wildness of the anecdotes she told me, there was a very real possibility that without her constant intervention and watch, he could have died months before he did. For that, I am forever grateful to her and their entire friend group.

At the end of the day, it was Tyler who was relapsing, not me, my mom, or any of his college friends. While addiction is a disease, and Tyler's struggles were many and intense, he ultimately did not tell those who could have helped that he was having problems again. In high school, he raised his hand and asked for our assistance when he felt himself spiraling out of control. This action reassured us that, should it ever get to a scary point again, he would once again sound the alarm before he went too far. I don't know if he was scared to repeat the cycle of recovery, or maybe just didn't feel that he had hit rock bottom yet. Whatever the case, he did not ask for help this time. He continued to lie and hide his relapse from us, getting better at the concealment all the while.

I'd like to believe that he was going to ask for help at some point, that the fentanyl-laced pill was a freak accident, purely bad luck, that his problem wasn't *that* serious. I don't know anymore, though. I think Tyler was confident in what he was doing, that he could stop before anything too crazy happened, and that confidence made him unable to recognize the precariousness of his own situation. I don't think he ever really thought he could die, and neither did any of the friends who saw him relapsing.

The fact also remains that Tyler had deep-seated issues that caused him to seek out ways to "turn his brain off," his own words for the effect he so desired when he tried drugs. He wanted to feel normal, and no amount of addiction therapy or reasoning could stop the ceaseless torrent in his head. Carmen and Avery certainly couldn't stop him from experiencing anxiety, nor could they see inside his head and know exactly which behaviors were in good fun and which were a disastrous coping mechanism.

So, what to do with this mixed bag of stories and the questions of guilt and blame? I have at some point blamed myself, my parents, Tyler, his friends, and his drug dealer for his death, but I keep circling back to the point that *he is dead*. No matter who ultimately is responsible, or how many warning signs there were, the event remains irreversible. Nobody, Tyler included, thought he would or wanted him to die. So many things can change the course of events, and at this point, I find it pointless to try to pinpoint the exact moments where he might have been saved. I also recognize how many times we *did* save him, how this moment could have happened at fourteen, sixteen, or seventeen years old.

I don't know which is worse, to be honest—to think that Tyler was always doomed to die young or that we could have saved him. There is no point in playing the what-if game; because either way, he is gone. All we can do is be thankful for the nineteen years that he did have and recognize that each and every one of us played a part in achieving that. I am so grateful that in his final year of life, he got to experience the excitement of college, the joy of making new friends who really cared about him, and felt the hope for a long, healthy future.

XV

———

Like most people around the world, March 2020 sent Tyler, Lauren, Courtney, and I home from our respective institutions to wait out the COVID-19 quarantine. My three siblings were in college, and while I had already graduated, I was living alone in Sacramento, California, and did not want to spend quarantine utterly disconnected from any human contact. The four of us flew back to northern Virginia and fell into a lifestyle similar to what existed before any of us left for college. It was nice, actually—for a few months I was surrounded by my entire family for the first time in years. I was working remotely as the other three were finishing their semester online, and we all adjusted fairly well to the sudden lack of personal space that life in our parents' house afforded.

Tyler took up summer classes and started driving for Instacart, a grocery delivery service that allows drivers to make extra money on their own schedule, similar to Uber. My mom and I shared a similar relief at him being in the house instead of all the way in Chicago. We could watch over him a little more closely, both academically and regarding his substance abuse. The truth is that we still didn't trust him at all, and the few months he spent on his own in college terrified us. Even though we didn't know about the truth of his college relapses yet, we certainly had our suspicions.

Things seemed okay, though. Tyler was earning some money and staying busy, both positive signs that he was making progress and staying out of trouble. His grades were slightly better than those of his first semester and he seemed to be sober. He reconnected with some younger friends he knew from high school and started spending time with a new crowd. The sudden appearance of unknown friends was a red flag to us, but not enough to intervene. Tyler was now nineteen years old, past the age where my mom could stamp out less than ideal friendships by refusing to drive him to his playdate. He continued working and socializing normally for a few months and the balance between worry and trust seemed, for a while, to reach a state of livable homeostasis.

We especially felt at ease because of Tyler's declaration to switch majors from chemical engineering to math. When he first entered college, he thought chemical engineering would be the most profitable major for him after graduation, when he hoped to work with the chemistry of artificial food coloring and flavoring. Despite the seemingly idyllic combination of his passions for chemistry and math, he quickly fell behind in school. He struggled in his chemical engineering classes, earning all Ds and one B his first semester.

These bad grades were frightening because of their potential cause: drugs. Tyler vehemently reassured us it was a simple misalignment of interests. Math was his real passion, and it did not take long for him to realize that chemical engineering was not as math heavy as he was hoping. He enjoyed the labs and hands-on work, but he preferred complex, theoretical math to the chemistry coursework of balancing equations without a real-life application. In fact, the only thing keeping him off the academic probation list was the accumulation of credits he entered college with from community college math courses he took before and during his time in rehab. His GPA was not high enough after the first semester to formally switch majors. Nonetheless, he could still take any math classes he wanted as electives. He planned to use those classes to simultaneously improve his grades and knock out math major requirements. This dedicated plan for the future and attitude of seriousness toward his studies calmed our anxieties about his poor performance thus far.

He was maintaining friendships, appearing to stay sober, and showing a genuine interest in improving his grades and planning for the future. To us who had seen the worst, Tyler seemed happier and more stable than he had been in years.

One night, the two of us were working in our basement together, me sending out some work emails, him writing an essay for his English class. He droned on about how annoyed he was at our mom for constantly asking about his schoolwork and checking his grades in the online student portal.

"To be fair, you did fail four out of five of your classes last semester," I pointed out.

"Yeah, but that's because I wasn't used to college and I'm in the wrong major. I have a plan now," he retorted, frustrated that I didn't trust his commitment to school. It was the first time I ever saw him motivated to make a true effort to improve, and this sentiment gave me hope that he might be finally moving on from his static period of bad grades and substance abuse.

The cracks began to show about a month before he died. My mom caught him one night completely fucked up on Xanax, trying to sneak food up to his room. He could barely form a sentence and was so uncoordinated that he tried to eat a spoonful of ice cream and literally missed his mouth. My mom was mortified and told him she was going to take him to the emergency room. This set alarm bells off even in his fogged-up brain. He was adamant that he was all right, he just needed to go to sleep. She walked him upstairs where she became even more horrified. There, on one of his chairs, was a Ziploc bag full of crushed Sharpie ink tubes. She assumed he was using it to inhale but couldn't get a clear answer as to what the hell it was before he passed out. He was completely unconscious the moment he hit the bed despite her attempts to wake him. She was petrified that he would stop breathing. She checked on him several times throughout the night, yet the next day he was totally fine.

When asked once again about the bag of Sharpies, all he said was, "I don't remember." He had been so out of his mind high that he had no clue whether or not he had huffed Sharpies. She was petrified, but he firmly claimed that it was a one-time thing; he had just taken Xanax with some friends because he was having a bad day. It had not happened before and would not happen again.

This incident took me back to the first time we saw him relapse after he left rehab. It was the day before New Year's Eve, and I was the one who found him. Between his first and second semesters of college, our family rented an Airbnb in Chicago for the holidays, virtually hosting a weeklong party. Social drinking, pool playing, and gambling isn't exactly a recipe for success for an addict in recovery, but Tyler was handling it with grace. I was later told that that night in particular, most of the adults seemed overtly intoxicated. I went to bed early and had no idea what was transpiring. Tyler and I were sharing a room, and I was asleep for a few hours when I was woken by the unmistakable sound of vomiting.

"Tyler?" I sat up in bed, groggy, unsure of what I had just heard. Was I dreaming?

"Yep," he replied calmly and casually in the complete darkness.

"Did you just...throw up?" I asked, incredibly confused and trying to find my glasses.

"It's all good!" he chuckled, not answering my question.

"Are you okay?" I was now wide awake; sure something was wrong.

"How about another round of two-hand draw?" was his response.

I jumped to my feet and turned on the lights. There he was, lying in bed, a jet of pink vomit sprayed out in front of his face across the pillows. He was not quite asleep but was lying there nonchalantly and giggling as I tried to make sense of what was happening.

At this point it was almost 5:00 a.m. I darted into my mom's room, pounding on the door. She got out of bed when she saw me crying, barely able to relay what was happening in the other room.

"Tyler's drunk," I sniffed. "Like, trashed."

She didn't say a word following me into the bedroom, where he was still lying in the same position. She and Jeff got him washed off, threw the dirty pillowcases in the laundry, and set a trash can at his bedside. He was way too drunk to understand what was going on or to tell us what happened, but the next day he revealed that he waited until around 4:00 a.m. when everyone went to bed and began chugging everything he could find. He must have drunk close to a fifth of various liquors and was miserably ill the entire next day.

His reasoning for why he did it was unclear, even to him. I don't pretend to know what was happening in his head. I

imagine it had something to do with the weeklong temptation of alcohol around him paired with the stress of having
just told our mom the week prior that he failed most of his
classes. Regardless of the reason, it exacerbated our constant
worry about what might have been happening while he was
miles away in school. If he was relapsing right in front of his
entire family, who knows what he was doing when he was
unchaperoned at college in another state?

Both times he relapsed, we had a serious conversation
about his sobriety and offered him the same resources we
had before. He knew that returning to a recovery program
was always an option but reassured us that this was nowhere
near how bad things were when he first went to rehab. Yet
that last summer, just like that holiday season, there was no
way to know the true extent of his issues, and all we could
do was be there for him. He seemed fine most of the time,
keeping up with work and spending time with both sides of
the family. Surely if he were spiraling downward, he wouldn't
be keeping it together so well, right?

After he died, I uncovered the extent of the spiral through
one of the new, suspicious friends he had been spending
time with, Kyle. Kyle had his own history with substance
abuse—he used to be addicted to pills, mostly downers like
Xanax, and one day he stole money from a charity car wash
he participated in at summer camp to pay for his addiction.
When he got caught, he finally confessed to his parents that
he needed help and began intensive outpatient therapy.

The pair first started spending time together because Tyler
heard through a mutual friend that Kyle had a fake ID, so
they met up to buy alcohol and struck up a companionship
that involved seeing each other multiple days a week. Kyle
knew Tyler's story as well, mentioning that Tyler was sober

when they first started hanging out. Only later did he show up while on Xanax. Kyle wasn't sure when or why Tyler started using pills again, but Tyler continued to do Percocet or Xanax from that day on while Kyle would smoke weed and not ask questions.

Kyle described Tyler's attitude toward drugs that summer as somewhat controlled. When they first started hanging out, Tyler talked about how he had been clean for a long time, so when he started taking pills again, it wasn't a big deal. Tyler specifically told him to not let him take pills if he was already drinking and seemed to have an air of knowing what he was doing or at least caring about how far he went. Especially since Tyler had such an extensive knowledge of the chemistry of drugs, Kyle defaulted to trusting his judgment and avoiding confrontation. Kyle continued to steer clear of anything hard himself, but he never questioned Tyler's choices. He, too, had experienced the hardships of addiction and thought it would only add to Tyler's pain if he challenged his decisions or gave him a hard time while he was going through a rough patch.

"Do you think I'm more fun when I'm fucked up or sober?" Tyler asked him one day, explaining that he felt as if he was a better person when on drugs. They calmed the torrent of uncontrollable thoughts that plagued his mind every day of his life.

"I guess it just depends on the mood or situation," Kyle replied, not wanting to give a definitive answer either way.

After Tyler died, I asked Kyle why he thought Tyler started using again.

"He felt better physically and mentally," he explained. "He was very upset and frustrated and anxious when he was sober; he was a lot more relaxed on drugs. Anyone who is frustrated and has symptoms of trying to overcome addiction isn't doing well and isn't as fun. He was more fun when he was fucked up, who wouldn't be?"

Tyler's substance use quickly moved from fun to scary, however. Tyler came to pick Kyle up one night and was completely blasted. He was swerving on the road, almost crashing the car. He asked Kyle to pay for his Wendy's one day, admitting that he had squandered all his Instacart earnings on drugs, yet managed to make excuses for the situation, acting as if he had everything under control. Kyle recognized the mindset of the addicted, the complete disassociation with reality and self-awareness, and empathized with what was now clearly a problem once more.

Another one of their mutual friends, Rich, had been the main supplier of Tyler's pills the entire summer. Rich was sixteen years old, lived in the next county, and other friends of Tyler said he sold pills to many customers in the area. Tyler would often give Rich a ride in exchange for pills since he didn't have his license yet or just buy them with cash. He would often tell our mom that he was going to run some Instacart orders, then use his genius brain to scramble the GPS locator on his phone and drive to Rich's house.

The pill that killed him was purchased from Rich, and from texts and conversations with friends, Tyler seemed to think it was a Percocet stamped with something stronger. The toxicology report, however, stated that the only substance in his body at the time of death was fentanyl. While confusing, these mixed reports are actually very in line with the current state of the illegal drug market.

If there is one thing you take away from this book, please let it be this: fentanyl is horrifying. It is a fairly new phenomenon in the United States, but I firmly believe that once media catches on it will be considered a full-fledged national crisis. It has always been possible to lace illegal drugs with other substances. Fentanyl, though, is a new and extremely lethal element. Addicts and non-addicts alike are dying of overdose in terrifying numbers, often from an event as trivial as trying something fun at a college party.

In 2019, the National Association of Boards of Pharmacy, National Association of Drug Diversion Investigators, and Partnership for Safe Medicines released a study detailing the alarming spike in the use of pill presses to make counterfeit medications, especially with fentanyl. Pill presses are legal to buy and largely unregulated, which means even the most inexperienced drug dealer can obtain one. Cheaply imported fentanyl, an opioid fifty to one hundred times stronger than morphine, is pressed into the fake pills to create a stronger high for less money, creating huge profits for dealers (National Association of Boards of Pharmacy, 2019).

Basically, dealers say they are selling genuine Percocet or other prescription painkillers, which can be expensive and hard to obtain in large quantities since they must be ordered by a doctor. Dealers make a fake pill with little or no actual amount of the painkiller and add fentanyl, which is cheaper and extremely potent even in miniscule amounts. The fake pill is in many cases even stronger than the painkiller it is masquerading as, addicting users more quickly and giving them stronger highs, which builds a huge and loyal clientele. In fact, rumors of a customer who overdosed and died can actually *increase* a drug dealer's sales because addicted users know that the dealer's stock is strong (Macy, 2018).

Tyler knew that the pill he was buying was not a normal Percocet. What he did not expect was the lethal dose of fentanyl that ultimately ended his life. The day before he died,

Rich told him, "Be careful with this shit. I overdosed on it, but I'm fine now." Tyler himself had taken something from the same sale the day before, and said it was the best he ever had. It is unclear if Rich was taking the same types of pills, or if Tyler had already taken one fentanyl pill and survived, but the two of them trying and enjoying similar pills gave him a sense of security.

Tyler took his last pill before bed, though, using the mystery pill to go to sleep after a particularly frustrating day. Before he went to bed, he talked with my mom for a while. He mentioned that he was overthinking the argument he had with Stella, so we wonder if he took the pill specifically to reduce the hyperactivity in his brain. Since fentanyl is a depressant, it is likely that Tyler simply fell asleep before he even noticed any signs of overdose. Fentanyl can slow or stop breathing altogether, which is most likely what occurred, since Tyler was not found with any other signs of overdose (e.g., aspiration or foaming at the mouth). The autopsy revealed swelling in the brain, consistent with fatal hypoxia, the condition of the brain not receiving enough oxygen. (National Institute on Drug Abuse, 2021).

When Kyle got the phone call, he was smoking with some friends in a park, and thought his friend was making a cruel joke, fucking with him while he was high. He hadn't heard from Tyler all day, and when the friend on the phone assured him that this was real, he blurted the news out to those around him, and they all fell silent.

"I walked over to the side of the pavilion," Kyle told me. "I looked psycho, I was talking to the sky, to his energy. I told him, 'You're an idiot, man. You could have just not taken it.'"

Kyle, like Tyler, had felt no real danger because of the combination of the God complex and Tyler's own genius.

Someone who had been experimenting with drugs for almost a decade and who was a master of math and chemistry could surely keep his measurements correct and never get into too much danger. Right? I don't think Kyle, or Tyler, or I, or anyone, thought that Tyler could get it that wrong. We always thought that the same hyperactive, genius brain that got him into this mess could get him out just as easily.

Something Kyle and I both confronted after Tyler's death was a sort of universal God complex, or main character syndrome, that just about every person alive was guilty of possessing. No one *actually* feels like they can die; we all know it can happen, *will* inevitably happen, but we don't truly internalize that in a conscious sense. We are the only point of view we have ever known, so how could that end? Premature, freak deaths only seemed to happen to a friend of a friend. To be suddenly punched in the face with the death of a person we were so close to and was part of our everyday life gave both of us a startling sense of our own mortality. If a healthy nineteen-year-old could drop dead with no warning, certainly so could we.

I remember hearing about his death from the police for the first time, thinking how bizarre the words sounded were in relation to my brother. "Autopsy" and "brain swelling" were terms previously only encountered on episodes of *Law & Order*, but now they were being used to describe someone I know and love. A pervading cloud of confusion still follows me, even months after his death. This isn't the kind of thing that happens to people. How is it happening to me? To Tyler? To our family? It continues to feel unreal, even when I talk about it. Hearing the words come out of my own mouth, I had the sensation that I was describing something I heard on a murder podcast.

The events following Tyler's death were similarly difficult for me to process. As the detectives on Tyler's case explained to our family, drug prosecutions are extremely difficult procedures. First and foremost, there are rarely any cooperative witnesses. If a lethal overdose triggers the investigation, as in Tyler's case, the star witness is already dead and other customers are unlikely to talk since exposing their dealer means they risk getting in trouble or their supply will be cut off. The best source of evidence at police disposal is cell phones but warrants for social media data are hard to come by and sometimes end up not being useful. Companies like Snapchat and Facebook do store data. Their size, however, means that a warrant could take six months to process.

Then there are hierarchies. At the lowest levels, most street dealers are users themselves. They are supplied by someone else, who is supplied by someone else, on and on up the chain. The demand is so high that catching a low-level dealer often does virtually nothing to solve the larger problem as another addict who is strapped for cash will typically take over the old dealer's territory immediately. Plus, even if a street dealer is caught, it is extremely unlikely that their sources can be traced all the way up to a manufacturer, sometimes five or six degrees removed. At each level there must be witnesses and absolute proof of an illegal drug sale, making it nearly impossible to successfully kill the drug supplying hydra.

These facts were extremely disheartening to hear from the person in charge of Tyler's case. I felt hopeless knowing the people most capable of apprehending the dealers involved in Tyler's death were not confident in a positive outcome. Kyle and I were both dismayed at the realization that there probably will not be justice for Tyler. It is a weird feeling, having your entire world destroyed but having no way to seek reparations for it. Without much in the way of legal ramifications, the only ways to truly do much about fentanyl-related deaths must occur before the overdose happens.

The first and most obvious prevention tool is drug education. While this seems like a no-brainer because of how recently fentanyl entered the illegal drug scene, knowledge of its potency and frequency in illegal drugs is widely unknown. The threat of a fentanyl overdose overshadows most other potential dangers of illegal drugs, and many have died without even knowing what fentanyl is. Anything can contain fentanyl: cocaine, heroin, "prescription" pills, meth—you name it. Many friends and family members I talked to about Tyler's death had no clue about fentanyl until this tragedy forced them to learn.

The second is drug testing kits. There are kits online that use chemical reactors to determine if a drug is laced with fentanyl. For those suffering from addiction who are not yet in recovery, this could be a life-saving purchase. Testing kits are not perfect remedies, though—because it takes so little fentanyl, sometimes near-microscopic amounts, to kill someone, a test could miss a tiny but lethal flake of fentanyl floating in a larger amount of powder or liquid (Partnership to End Addiction, 2019).

Finally, Narcan, or naloxone, works as an opioid antagonist and can save a person who is in the middle of an overdose. Narcan is an over-the-counter medicine that can be purchased from a pharmacy, and many community organizations offer training classes that teach you how to administer Narcan to a person in crisis. Having Narcan in a home, car, or purse first-aid kit could save someone's life in the critical moments before an ambulance arrives.

It is too late to save my little brother. Tyler's addiction overrode his better judgment, and he was alone when he took a fentanyl-laced pill and overdosed. Those of us who remain have a duty to learn from his story and take real, immediate action to do slow the stream of fentanyl deaths in our own communities until larger government and health programs step in to help eradicate the problem on a larger scale.

XVI

So, Tyler, how did I do? Are you proud of me?

I wish you were here to give me your opinion, but by the time mom called me and I was on the floor screaming it was already too late. I can't bring you back no matter how hard I try. I wrote this stupid book to try to keep you here as much as possible. You're still gone, though. I could document every moment of your life and win a Pulitzer Prize and it still wouldn't change a thing.

That's the hardest part about this: you're always gone every second of every day. The guilt and anger come and go but what remains constant is your absence. You never come back. Even when all the negative feelings subside for a while and I'm just remembering the good stuff, you're still gone. More than anything else, I just miss you so badly. There's an emptiness in my life every day that no amount of time or healing can fix. There's no other you, there's no replacement or consolation prize.

The emptiness isn't just a hole or a missing piece, it's *me*. You are not just a part of me, you *are* me. Scientifically, biologically, genetically, I am you. You and I share the same blood from the same two people. But your blood, my blood, our blood, was drained and replaced with formaldehyde before they stuffed you in a box and buried you in the ground.

I had to look at your body. Your *body*. Without you in it. You were there but you weren't. I have intrusive thoughts, waking nightmares, about the way your hands felt. They weren't you. They weren't the same hands that pulled my hair when we were little or that hugged me when we were adults, saying goodbye every time I left to go back to California.

How could you do that to me? How could you make me see that? How could you leave me? I needed you. I still need you. I don't know how to be Alexis without Tyler. You made me everything I am today, were a part of every single thing that I am. I'm not mad at you, but fuck, am I mad at you. You took away the person I love most in the entire world. If you weren't already dead, I'd fucking kill you for doing this to the person I love more than anything. I know you didn't mean to do it and you didn't mean to make me so horrifically sad. Still, you did, and you're not even here to help me through it.

I'm going insane without you. Everybody always asks me, "How's your mom?" But how the hell am I? I just lost the only person who was there for me my entire life. I don't have children; you were the thing I loved most, the strongest bond I had on this Earth. You were the only person who knew me before the divorce, before we even moved to Virginia, the only person who went back and forth between houses with me, saw every moment and knew it all. Even our parents only saw half of our lives—it was always you and me. We have been through every single thing together and now I'm just supposed to keep going on with my life alone? I don't know how to. I don't know who I am without you.

I don't know what to call us, kindred spirits? Twin flames? We were something special. You understood everything about me almost telepathically, my issues and the genetic problems that we shared. We both have anxiety issues, yours were just worse—I can live with mine; they aren't an all-consuming nightmare. We'd make fun of mom when she told us to calm down or stop freaking out like, "Thanks, Julie! I didn't realize I could just choose not to be anxious!" And now I am by myself with all our genetic oopsies that make everyday life really fucking hard. No one I know understands what I have to live with constantly, the hyperactive worrying and inability to turn it off or just enjoy life for a while.

I'm just so tired of "being strong." I don't want to be strong; I want to kick around on the floor and scream. I want to break things and yell at people and lock myself in my room forever because I don't know how this life can still possibly be worth living. Right when you died, I thought about it for a minute, thought about ending it all because I didn't know if any of it would be worth it without you.

I want to keep going but I still don't really know how. How do I get married with an empty spot in my bridal party? The best day of my life will be ruined. How do I raise my kids without an uncle? I never told you this: you completely ruined my college graduation day. You were supposed to come before you got in trouble at rehab and mom didn't think it was best for you to fly out anymore, so she cancelled your trip. Through wishful thinking I convinced myself she was just surprising me—surely there was no way you wouldn't be there for me; miss the most important thing I've ever done. Then I was walking down the Lawn, arm in arm with some of my best friends, and when I walked past the whole family cheering me on, you weren't there. I lost it, cried through the whole ceremony, and that was when you were still alive. How do I keep seeing that empty space at every happy event for the rest of my life and not let it ruin the whole day? What's the point of doing all these accomplishments if I can't share them with the most important person in my entire life?

I want to publish this book and get a PhD with our last name on it (there's no doubt in my mind you would have gotten one, you're so damn smart) and take care of mom and get married and name a kid after you but the more things I do the farther away from you I get. I just want to sit still. I didn't want to celebrate New Year's 2021 because even though 2020 was the worst year of my life, I didn't want to be living in a year you never lived in. I don't want to be forty-five and have you still be nineteen years old. I don't want to tell people that I had a brother once who died when we were younger. I want you to grow up with me, alongside me. I want us to get old and wrinkly together and share our fulfilling lives by each other's side. Now I have to grow up by myself and one day go to mom's funeral alone.

One day I will have lived more of my life without you than with you, and you will not have been around for so many important moments. I will grow and change and not be able to talk to you about any of it. It terrifies me beyond my own wits to think that someday I won't feel close to you anymore like I do right now. Even right now, you don't know that I'm going back to grad school or writing an entire book about you.

It's unfair, Tyler, it's so unfair. Anything could have happened to me, anything but this. There isn't a single pain I wouldn't bear to have you back or a single person I wouldn't trade (myself included). This is the worst thing that has ever happened to me and that will probably ever happen to me. Even so, it's also way worse for you and I just feel so sad for you. You deserved so much, you had the kindest heart, the most giving soul, you had the genius to change the entire world. You don't even get to graduate college or have babies or experience the real world or travel or live the life you deserve. I'm so sorry I couldn't help you, Tyler. I want to give you the whole world but now you have nothing.

Other people will move on and forget about you. I won't. I will always be broken, less than I was before, half of my former self. It hurts, Tyler, it hurts so badly I don't know what to do with all of it. Every day in the kitchen I expect you to stomp down the stairs and say, "Hey Lecky," and show me some obscure YouTube video I don't understand. I just sit at your grave and stare at it; I want to dig you out and save you. I keep having these dreams where I find out it's all fake; you're actually alive and it was some elaborate government ruse. They're worse than nightmares because then I wake up and I realize you're gone all over again. It just keeps hitting me in the face over and over. Sometimes I'll even be awake, doing something completely normal and it'll hit me then, as if I didn't already know. I'll have a full-on panic attack as if I'm just now realizing you're gone, no matter how long it's been. It continues to hurt and surprise me. I didn't expect it to still hurt this bad almost a year later. It just isn't getting better.

I'm torn between the absolute despair and hopelessness versus the urge to fight on even harder for you. Since you've died, I've gotten into grad programs, moved across the country, and written an entire book all while working full time. Your death has motivated me in ways I can't even describe; it's like I have to keep moving and doing and succeeding at all times or else I'm failing you, or else it's all for nothing. I feel like I have to work doubly hard; I have to do double the number of things in my lifetime so that I can make up for all that you don't get to do. I know that's not true, that's not a healthy way to think, but I would just feel so awful if you were dead and I were a failure. We're so much more than that and I have to do it for us. The least I can do is create a legacy for you, keep your name alive and try to give mom and dad enough pride and joy for two kids. They were so, so proud of you and always will be. Still, there was so much more you were supposed to do, so much more they were going to be proud of.

I won't let your death only be a loss, I won't. I won't let people only remember Tyler Joe Young as a tragedy. Your memorial fund will save someone else's life. This book will keep your memory alive and close, and you'll live forever in these pages and with everyone who reads this. Everything I do will be partially credited to you because you were the strongest, bravest person I know. If I could embody even a fraction of the drive you had to get better and fight addiction, I'll be able to live a life overflowing with love and accomplishments. You were my baby brother, but I really looked up to you and couldn't imagine how you were able to handle as much as you did. I think of myself when I was nineteen, how immature and inexperienced I was. I'm thankful that you were so much more than I was; because if I had died at nineteen, I wouldn't have done anything half as inspiring as you did.

I just want to make you proud. I know that compared to you I'm the dumb kid in the family, but I want to prove that I am indeed related to you, that *most*, not quite *all* of the intelligence went to you. I don't know where you are, but I want you to look down on me and smile, knowing I'm carrying the torch for you and our family. I won't let you down. I can't. Now I sometimes think about the possibility that I could die at any time, today, tomorrow, at any moment just like you did. You were a healthy nineteen-year-old and now you're gone at the drop of the hat. Who's to say I'll live to a ripe old age? There's truly no time to waste. I am mourning you every single day, and I'm trying to make it motivate me, too. There are days when I can barely get out of bed, and those are the times I feel the worst because I know I'm not doing what you would want for me.

The other side of all this is a complete black hole, a bottomless pit of sadness and nothingness that I am running myself thin to avoid. When I think of what your death really means for my own life it completely consumes me, becomes the only thing that has ever mattered. Sometimes I'm so overwhelmed, I put all this pressure on myself to make it all mean something, but it's all I can do. Everybody tells me they can't believe how well I'm handling everything or how strong I'm being, but they don't see me crying myself to sleep every night, crying so hard I throw up sometimes. I just miss you so fucking much. I'm so exhausted from fighting through this sadness all the time, yet if I stopped and just chilled out for a while and let myself wallow, I'd be even sadder because I'd be wasting the potential, the opportunities to make the rest of my life matter for you. That's why I keep going, keep channeling that weird genetic inability to sit still into progress that means something.

I just wish I could know if I'm doing it right. I know there's no "right" way to grieve, but I want to make the most of your life and death and make sure that no matter what happens next, you are never forgotten. You know how I always write letters—it's the best way I can think of to express how much I love someone. I guess this is just one big love letter for the most important love I've ever known. Do you remember your fifteenth birthday when I got hundreds of different people to text you happy birthday? I want this to be like that. I want all these people, some who knew you, some who didn't, to think about and celebrate you. I want people who love you to read this with fondness, and I want those who didn't to read this and wish they'd gotten the chance to meet you. I also certainly can't live without you, so I have to take you with me wherever I go. If I do become forty-five one day and feel myself growing away from you, I need to have this as undeniable proof of how much you mean to me and how we will never truly be apart.

We are a team forever whether we're alive or dead, and it's my turn to carry the team. When I come and join you one day, I want to know that I've done everything I can to memorialize you, to help others avoid your fate, and to do enough for us both to be fulfilled. That's my promise to you. You will not have died in vain—everything I do will be because of you or for you for the rest of my life. You've been the best brother I could ever ask for, and now it's my turn to do a few things in return. I just wish you were here to see them.

I feel you watching over me sometimes. There are these moments where I'm outside and it's quiet and if I close my eyes, I know you're standing there next to me. Maybe I sound crazy. I don't really care, though, because that's all I have anymore. If I think too hard about the fact that I'll never hug you again for the rest of my life, I freak out. I don't know how to move forward but I'm trying, Tyler. Just stay with me, please. Be my guardian angel and give me signs that I'm doing a good job.

So, thank you, Tyler, for always making me a better version of myself no matter where you are. Thank you for being my rock during every challenge life has ever thrown at me. Thank you for sending me butterflies and spiders to let me know that you're still with me. Thank you for showing me that we are still worthy of love and capable of amazing things even though we can't get our brains to shut up sometimes. Thank you for all the *Star Wars* facts, all the internet challenges, the math problems, the trombone and piano concerts, the YouTube videos, the boy advice, the friendship, the best thing I've ever experienced. Thank you for letting me be your big sister for nineteen years and forever.

ACKNOWLEDGMENTS

I doubt anyone has ever written a book alone, but I had an especially large team who made this particular book possible. In the wake of my worst nightmare coming true, it took every ounce of strength I had to get out of bed every morning and try to write something worthwhile to honor my brother. *All* that strength came from those around me who supported and cheered me on when I couldn't find enough motivation within myself. You really don't know how much love is in your life until it's time to rally the troops, and boy, did they rally. My heart is overflowing, even at a time when I feel so empty.

First, thank you to Tyler Joe Young. Without you, there is no book, and there is no me. You not only gave me a book's worth of subject matter, but you also helped shape me into who I am today. I would have neither the means nor the motivation to write this book if I were not blessed to have you as my brother. I hope you feel that this book does justice to your brief but incredible life and are smiling down on me from wherever you are. I love you with all my being.

Second, thank you to my wonderful family. We've been through hell together, and I hope this book gives you a little bit of peace and a way to remember what we lost. The hole in our family will be there forever, but you all ease the pain just a little bit. To my momma, my dad, Lindsey, Jeff, Hudson, Courtney, Connor, Dalton, Lauren, and Briley, thank you all for loving Tyler and working together to help him until the very end.

Next, thank you to those who loved Tyler enough to share their stories with me. You helped me learn more about this person I love and miss so dearly and added priceless memories to this book. Without you, I would only be able to write about Tyler as a little brother instead of the entirety of the man he came to be: Tim Miller, Phil Miller, Joyce Carr, Zaina Salman, Madelyn Cummins, Tom Anders, Steve Toby, Marcus Kneitz, Mel Hefty, Aidan Johnson, and Katie McMullen.

I would also like to thank the folks at the Creator Institute and New Degree Press for the opportunity of a lifetime. Thank you for kicking my butt into being a better writer and giving me the tools to create a memorial for my brother.

Finally, an enormous thank you to those who made this book possible by committing to reading it and keeping Tyler's memory alive: Michelle Wilson, Kathy Grillo, Chioma Obaji, Kylie Woloshyn, the Tiger Family, Matt Garvin, Jessa Oliveira, Michelle Kim, Lily Henderson, Mike Tekin, Forest Saunders, Krista Long, the Rose Family, Morgan Harrison, Cassie Rossi, Meredith Fahey, Saige McGovern, Courtney Matsuo, Sue Vinci, Lisa Andrusyszyn, Chris Miller, Kat Jackson, Suchi Patel, Crystal Birnie, Eddie McGlamery, Greg Lindgren, Matt Steelberg, Jake Henson, De'Vante Cross, Kevin Hirschfield, Alicia Anderson, Rachel Legard, Sarah Winn, Nathan Kamm, Rebecca Gallagher, Sarah Piszczor, Ian Linville, Amy Lourenco, Krista Ferraro, Brielle Truong, Donna Vitalie, Kent Young, Tiffanie Chau-Dang, Magdalena Anders, Nick Ferraro, Shelley Skocaj, Logan Quinn, Bob

Miller, Chad Whych, Katrina Miller-Stevens, Bryn Hanharan, Pat Miller, the Hoover Family, Murad Mahmood, Sandra Yokum, Kim Meyers, the Damuth Family, the Keedy Family, Rebecca Clar, the Rodriguez Family, Mallory Parker, Brigid Duffy, Patrick O'Hara, Mary Paquette, Jennifer Parry, Jane McGuire, Anna Giddins, Michael Smith, Millie Ouk, Julie Jacobs, Dave Boyd, Julie Campbell, Lourdes Blanco, Rob Gieser, Stephanie Dooley, Emily Cripps, Whitney Forstner, Greg Harris, Kara Tekel, Patrick Flaherty, Jennifer Giancola, Richard Heath, Megan Pickle, Sara Pearce, Jean Anfindsen, Kathleen Banashak, Tanya Larriva, the Bell Family, Susan Fraiman, Robyn Murphy, Donna Mullin, Ben Rogers, Erin Geiger, Charise Champagne, Christina Jones, Jayden Nixon, Natalie Hunt, Gabriella Dera, Madelyn Whitfield, Hojung Lee, Jocelyn Hsu, Tim Schott, Lodema Ronchetti, Jeff Jones, David McCallie, Austin Baney, Karrie Schweikert, Stephenie Henderson, Robert Slevin, Daniel Solomon, Kristie Pearmund, Carmen Critchlow, Karen Inglett, Jennifer Miller, TK Burton, Tom Maldrie, Kristi Miller, Lucy Long, Greg Mednik, Jane Kramer, Theresa Casey, Patricia Harkins, Margaret Michel, Melissa Prince, Jane Orem, Madeline McCombe, Cody Comer, Jerome Karnick, Stephanie Ducker, Charles Snowden, Cheryl Hines, Cheryl Hill, Teresa Diaz, Gwynnie Powers, Jessica Vasquez-Burns, Andrew Bacso, Phoebe Johnson, Karen Boyd, Scott Thornton, Julianna Orem, Rick Pappalardo, Gabrielle Kohlmeier, the D'Alessio Family, Regina Thomas, Tiffany Shum, Kelli Kellen, the Miranda Family, Renee Shertz, the Albrecht Family, Stephen Stern, Tori Hanway, Jess Miller, Nico Barton, Jessica Moskowitz, Thomas Wetherell, Linda Miller, Acara Miller, the Kendrat Family, Tracy Gordon, Eric Bremer, Alex McCord, Dow Phipps, Darwin Walter, Darota Rojek, Heather McCloskey, Daniel

Zambito, Trevor Cazares, Julie Edgcomb, Catherine Lancaster, Angelina Puglia, Tot Wood, Taylor Chevalier, Cheryl O'Neill, Kim Fedei, Glenn Catlett, Cyndi Jones, Magdalena Houck, the Bango Family, Jennifer Cato, Elizabeth Millinor, James Banks, Jane Decker, Rocio Escobedo, Melissa McCarthy, Stephanie Carver, Joe Reed, Ray Ramos, Michael Idzior, Heather Segersten, Jerri Hartz, Linda and Robert Phipps, Kim Young, Spencer Bozsik, Alena Latysheva, Lisa Vercauteren, Devin Holmes, Stacy Durand, RoseMarie Lee, and Christopher Souther.

APPENDIX

———

AUTHOR'S NOTE

Center for Disease Control and Prevention. "Fentanyl." Published February 16, 2021. https://www.cdc.gov/drugoverdose/opioids/fentanyl.html.

Macy, Beth. *Dopesick: Dealers, Doctors, and the Company That Addicted America*. New York, NY: Little, Brown and Company, 2018.

Mann, Brian. "Federal Judge Approves Landmark $8.3 Billion Purdue Pharma Opioid Settlement." *NPR*, November 18, 2020. https://www.npr.org/2020/11/17/936022386/federal-judge-ap-proves-landmark-8-3-billion-purdue-pharma-opioid-settle-ment.

CHAPTER 1

Beatty, Julia. "Baltimore: The Heroin Capital of the US." *Silverman Treatment Solutions; Addiction Medical Solutions, LLC*, July 21, 2016. https://silvermantreatment.com/baltimore-the-her-oin-capital-of-the-us/.

Hammersley, R., A. Forsyth, V. Morrison, and J.B. Davies. "The Relationship Between Crime and Opioid Use." *British Journal of Addiction*, 84, no. 9 (1989): 1029–1043. https://pubmed.ncbi. nlm.nih.gov/2790266/.

Macy, Beth. *Dopesick: Dealers, Doctors, and the Drug Company That Addicted America.* New York, NY: Little, Brown and Company, 2018.

CHAPTER 4

American Society for the Positive Care of Children. "Get The Facts: Adverse Childhood Experiences (ACES)." Accessed March 10, 2021. https://americanspcc.org/get-the-facts-adverse-child-hood-experiences/.

Fomby, Paula, and Andrew J. Cherlin. "Family Instability and Child Well-Being." *American Sociological Review* 27, no. 2 (2007): 181–204. https://pubmed.ncbi.nlm.nih.gov/21918579/.

National Institute on Drug Abuse. "Genetics and Epigenetics of Addiction DrugFacts." National Institutes of Health; U.S. Department of Health and Human Services, August 2019. https://www.drugabuse.gov/publications/drugfacts/genet-ics-epigenetics-addiction.

Sheff, David. *Beautiful Boy: A Father's Journey through His Son's Addiction.* Boston, MA: Houghton Mifflin, 2008.

Sheff, Nic. *Tweak: Growing up on Methamphetamines.* New York, NY: Simon & Schuster, 2008.

CHAPTER 5

Rapaport, Lisa. "Few U.S. Doctors Can Legally Prescribe Bubrenor-phine." *ACEP Now; American College of Emergency Physicians*, January 27, 2020. https://www.acepnow.com/article/few-u-s-doctors-can-legally-prescribe-bubrenorphine/.

Sheff, David. *Beautiful Boy: A Father's Journey through His Son's Addiction*. Boston, MA: Houghton Mifflin, 2008.

Substance Abuse and Mental Health Services Administration (US); Office of the Surgeon General (US). Facing Addiction in America: The Surgeon General's Report on Alcohol, Drugs, and Health [Internet]. Washington (DC): US Department of Health and Human Services; 2016 Nov. CHAPTER 6, HEALTH CARE SYSTEMS AND SUBSTANCE USE DISORDERS. Available from: https://www.ncbi.nlm.nih.gov/books/NBK424848/.

CHAPTER 6

Psychological Science, "Many People's Earliest Memories May Be Fictional." *Association for Psychological Science*, Published July 18, 2018. https://www.psychologicalscience.org/news/releases/many-peoples-earliest-memories-may-be-fictional.html.

Salek, Elyse C., and Kenneth R. Ginsburg. "How Children Under-stand Death & What You Should Say." *HealthyChildren.org. American Academy of Pediatrics*, September 11, 2014. https://www.healthychildren.org/English/healthy-living/emotion-al-wellness/Building-Resilience/Pages/How-Children-Un-derstand-Death-What-You-Should-Say.aspx.

CHAPTER 7

Sarkar, A. "Characteristics of Drug-Dependent People." *National Institute on Drug Abuse. US Department of Health and Human Services*, September 9, 2013. https://www.drugabuse.gov/international/abstracts/characteristics-drug-dependent-people.

Sheff, David. *Beautiful Boy: A Father's Journey through His Son's Addiction*. Boston, MA: Houghton Mifflin, 2008.

Sheff, Nic. *Tweak: Growing up on Methamphetamines*. New York, NY: Simon & Schuster, 2008.

CHAPTER 9

Cicero, Theodore J., Matthew S. Ellis, Hillary L. Surrat, and Steven P. Kurtz. "The Changing Face of Heroin Use in the United States: A Retrospective Analysis of the Past 50 Years." *JAMA Psychiatry.* 2014;71(7):821-826. doi:10.001/jamapsychiatry.2014.366.

Kosten, Thomas R, and Tony P. George. "The Neurobiology of Opioid Dependence: Implications for Treatment." *Sci Pract Perspect.* 2002; 1(1):13-20. doi:10.1151/sspo21113.

Levinson, Sam, dir. *Euphoria*. Special Episode, part 1, "Rue." Aired December 6, 2020, on HBO. https://www.hbomax.com/feature/urn:hbo:feature:GX7WPJgqYpLZJwwEAAABu.

Volkow, Nora. "Addressing the Stigma That Surrounds Addiction." *National Institute on Drug Abuse. US Department of Health and Human Services*, April 6, 2021. https://www.drugabuse.

gov/about-nida/noras-blog/2020/04/addressing-stigma-sur-
rounds-addiction.

CHAPTER 10

American Addiction Centers. "Treating Addiction with Anxiety
Disorders." Published February 3, 2020. https://americanad-
dictioncenters.org/anxiety-and-addiction.

Ashley Addiction Treatment. "Difference between Amphetamine
and Methamphetamine." Accessed January 10, 2020. https://
www.ashleytreatment.org/difference-between-amphet-
amine-and-methamphetamine/.

CHAPTER 14

Sack, David. "Why Relapse Isn't a Sign of Failure." *Psychology
Today,* October 19, 2012. https://www.psychologytoday.com/
us/blog/where-science-meets-the-steps/201210/why-relapse-
isnt-sign-failure.

Sheff, David. *Beautiful Boy: A Father's Journey through His Son's
Addiction.* Boston, MA: Houghton Mifflin, 2008.

CHAPTER 15

Illegal Pill Presses: An Overlooked Threat to American Patients.
Mount Prospect, IL: National Association of Boards of Pharmacy, National Association of Drug Diversion Investigators,
and The Partnership for Safe Medicines, 2019. https://nabp.
pharmacy/wp-content/uploads/2019/03/PillPress-WhitePa-
per-March2019.pdf.

Macy, Beth. *Dopesick: Dealers, Doctors, and the Drug Company That Addicted America*. New York, NY: Little, Brown and Company, 2018.

National Institute on Drug Abuse. "Fentanyl DrugFacts." National Institute on Drug Abuse; US Department of Health and Human Services, June 1, 2021. https://www.drugabuse.gov/publications/drugfacts/fentanyl.

Partnership to End Addiction. "What to Know about Drugs Laced with Fentanyl & Other Substances." Published July 2019. https://drugfree.org/article/what-to-know-about-drugs-laced-with-fentanyl-other-substances/.

Slowiczek, Lindsay. "Narcan: Dosage, Uses, Side Effects, How It Works, and More." *Medical News Today; MediLexicon International*, December 3, 2019. https://www.medicalnewstoday.com/articles/narcan#how-to-administer.

CPSIA information can be obtained
at www.ICGtesting.com
Printed in the USA
BVHW042212111021
618725BV00023B/660

9 781636 763712